I0752143

HENRY W. LONGFELLOW'S WRITINGS.

THE GOLDEN LEGEND. A Poem. Just Published. Price $1.00.

POETICAL WORKS. This edition contains the six Volumes mentioned below. In two volumes. 16mo. Boards. $2.00.

In separate Volumes, each 75 cents.

VOICES OF THE NIGHT.

BALLADS AND OTHER POEMS.

SPANISH STUDENT; A PLAY IN THREE ACTS.

BELFRY OF BRUGES, AND OTHER POEMS.

EVANGELINE; A TALE OF ACADIE.

THE SEASIDE AND THE FIRESIDE.

THE WAIF. A Collection of Poems. Edited by Longfellow.

THE ESTRAY. A Collection of Poems. Edited by Longfellow.

MR. LONGFELLOW'S PROSE WORKS.

HYPERION. A ROMANCE. Price $1.00.

OUTRE-MER. A PILGRIMAGE. Price $1.00.

KAVANAGH. A TALE. Price 75 cents.

Illustrated editions of THE POEMS and HYPERION.

NATHANIEL HAWTHORNE'S WRITINGS.

TWICE-TOLD TALES. Two Volumes. Price $1.50.

THE SCARLET LETTER. Price 75 cents.

THE HOUSE OF THE SEVEN GABLES. Price $1.00.

THE SNOW IMAGE, AND OTHER TWICE-TOLD TALES. Price 75 cents.

THE BLITHEDALE ROMANCE. Price 75 cents.

TRUE STORIES FROM HISTORY AND BIOGRAPHY. With four fine Engravings. Price 75 cents.

A WONDER-BOOK FOR GIRLS AND BOYS. With seven fine Engravings. Price 75 cents.

TANGLEWOOD TALES. Another 'Wonder-Book.' In press.

JOHN G. WHITTIER'S WRITINGS.

OLD PORTRAITS AND MOD. SKETCHES. Price 75 cents.

MARGARET SMITH'S JOURNAL. Price 75 cents.

SONGS OF LABOR, AND OTHER POEMS. Boards. 50 cts.

THE CHAPEL OF THE HERMITS. Cloth. 50 cents.

JAMES RUSSELL LOWELL'S WRITINGS.

COMPLETE POETICAL WORKS. Revised, with Additions. In two volumes, 16mo. Boards. Price $1.50.

SIR LAUNFAL. New Edition. Price 25 cents.

THE BIGLOW PAPERS. A New Edition. Price 63 cents.

EDWIN P. WHIPPLE'S WRITINGS.

ESSAYS AND REVIEWS. 2 Vols. Price $2.00.

LECTURES ON SUBJECTS CONNECTED WITH LITERATURE AND LIFE. Price 63 cents.

WASHINGTON AND THE REVOLUTION. Price 20 cts.

OLIVER WENDELL HOLMES'S WRITINGS.

POETICAL WORKS. With fine Portrait. Boards. $1.00.

ASTRÆA. Fancy paper. Price 25 cents.

GRACE GREENWOOD'S WRITINGS.

GREENWOOD LEAVES. 1st & 2d Series. $1.25 each.

POETICAL WORKS. With fine Portrait. Price 75 cents.

HISTORY OF MY PETS. With six fine Engravings. Scarlet cloth. Price 50 cents.

RECOLLECTIONS OF MY CHILDHOOD. With six fine Engravings. Scarlet cloth. Price 50 cents.

MRS. JUDSON'S WRITINGS.

ALDERBROOK. By Fanny Forester. 2 Vols. Price $1.75

THE KATHAYAN SLAVE, AND OTHER PAPERS. 1 vol. Price 63 cents.

HENRY GILES'S WRITINGS.

LECTURES, ESSAYS, AND MISCELLANEOUS WRITINGS. 2 Vols. Price $1.50.

DISCOURSES ON LIFE. Price 75 cents.

R. H. STODDARD'S WRITINGS.

POEMS. Cloth. Price 63 cents.

ADVENTURES IN FAIRY LAND. Just out. 75 cents.

WILLIAM MOTHERWELL'S WRITINGS.

POEMS, NARRATIVE AND LYRICAL. New Ed. $1.25.

POSTHUMOUS POEMS. Boards. Price 50 cents.

MINSTRELSY, ANC. AND MOD. 2 Vols. Boards. $1.50.

GOETHE'S WRITINGS.

WILHELM MEISTER. Translated by Thomas Carlyle. 2 Vols. Price $2.50.

GOETHE'S FAUST. Translated by Hayward. Price 75 cts.

MRS. CROSLAND'S WRITINGS.

LYDIA: A WOMAN'S BOOK. Cloth. 75 cents.

ENGLISH TALES AND SKETCHES. Cloth. $1.00.

MISCELLANEOUS.

CHARLES MACKAY'S POEMS. 1 Vol. Cloth. Price $1.00.

ROBERT BROWNING'S POETICAL WORKS. 2 Vols. $2.00.

HENRY ALFORD'S POEMS. Just out. Price $1.25.

RICHARD MONCKTON MILNES. POEMS OF MANY YEARS. Boards. Price 75 cents.

CHARLES SPRAGUE. POETICAL AND PROSE WRITINGS. With fine Portrait. Boards. Price 75 cents.

BAYARD TAYLOR. POEMS. Cloth. Price 63 cents.

HENRY T. TUCKERMAN. POEMS. Cloth. Price 75 cents.

JOHN G. SAXE. POEMS. With Portrait. Boards, 63 cents. Cloth, 75 cents.

BOWRING'S MATINS AND VESPERS. Price 50 cents.

REJECTED ADDRESSES. By HORACE and JAMES SMITH. Boards, Price 50 cents. Cloth, 63 cents.

WARRENIANA. A Companion to the 'Rejected Addresses.' Price 63 cents.

MEMORY AND HOPE. A BOOK OF POEMS, REFERRING TO CHILDHOOD. Cloth. Price $2.00.

JOSEPH T. BUCKINGHAM'S PERSONAL MEMOIRS AND RECOLLECTIONS OF EDITORIAL LIFE. With Portrait. 2 vols. 16mo. Price $1.50.

VILLAGE LIFE IN EGYPT. By the Author of 'Adventures in the Lybian Desert.' 2 vols. 16mo. Price $1.25.

PALISSY THE POTTER. By the Author of 'How to make Home Unhealthy.' 2 vols. 16mo. Price $1.50.

WILLIAM MOUNTFORD. THORPE: A QUIET ENGLISH TOWN, AND HUMAN LIFE THEREIN. 16mo. Price $1.00.

JAMES FREEMAN CLARKE. ELEVEN WEEKS IN EUROPE, AND WHAT MAY BE SEEN IN THAT TIME. 16mo. Price $1.00.

NOTES FROM LIFE. By HENRY TAYLOR, Author of 'Philip Van Artevelde.' 1 vol. 16mo. Price 63 cents.

THALATTA: A BOOK FOR THE SEA-SIDE. 1 vol. 16mo.

OUR VILLAGE. By MARY RUSSELL MITFORD. 2 vols. 16mo.

WILLIAM WORDSWORTH'S BIOGRAPHY. By Dr. C. WORDSWORTH. 2 Vols. Price $2.50.

MRS. A. C. LOWELL. THOUGHTS ON THE EDUCATION OF GIRLS. Price 25 cents.

CHARLES SUMNER. ORATIONS AND SPEECHES. 2 Vols. Price $2.50.

GEORGE S. HILLARD. THE DANGERS AND DUTIES OF THE MERCANTILE PROFESSION. Price 25 cents.

HORACE MANN. A FEW THOUGHTS FOR A YOUNG MAN. Price 25 cents.

F. W. P. GREENWOOD. SERMONS OF CONSOLATION. $1.00.

HEROINES OF THE MISSIONARY ENTERPRISE. 75 cts.

MEMOIR OF THE BUCKMINSTERS, FATHER AND SON. By Mrs. LEE. Price $1.25.

THE SOLITARY OF JUAN FERNANDEZ. By the Author of Picciola. Price 50 cents.

THE BOSTON BOOK. Price $1.25.

ANGEL-VOICES. Price 38 cents.

SIR ROGER DE COVERLEY. From the 'Spectator.' Price 75 cents.

S. T. WALLIS. SPAIN, HER INSTITUTIONS, POLITICS, AND PUBLIC MEN. Price $1.00.

RUTH, A New Novel by the Author of 'MARY BARTON.' Price 75 cents.

LABOR AND LOVE: A TALE OF ENGLISH LIFE. 50 cents.

EACH OF THE ABOVE POEMS AND PROSE WRITINGS, MAY BE HAD IN VARIOUS STYLES OF HANDSOME BINDING.

JUVENILE.

GRACE GREENWOOD'S

HISTORY OF MY PETS. A new and beautiful book, with six fine engravings. Square 16mo. Scarlet cloth, 50 cents.

RECOLLECTIONS OF MY CHILDHOOD. 50 cents.

NATHANIEL HAWTHORNE'S

TRUE STORIES FROM HISTORY AND BIOGRAPHY. With engravings. 16mo. Cloth gilt, 75 cents; cloth, gilt edge, $1.00.

WONDER-BOOK FOR GIRLS AND BOYS. With Engravings. 1 vol. 16mo. Cloth gilt, 75 cents; cloth, gilt edge, $1.00.

THE DESERT HOME, or, THE ADVENTURES OF A LOST FAMILY IN THE WILDERNESS. By Capt. Mayne Reid. With fine plates, $1.00.

THE BOY HUNTERS. By CAPT. REID. With fine plates. Just published.

ADVENTURES IN FAIRY LAND. By R. H. STODDARD. With fine plates. Just out. Price 75 cents.

AUNT EFFIE'S RHYMES. With beautiful Engravings. Just published. 75 cents.

ELIZA BUCKMINSTER LEE. FLORENCE, THE PARISH ORPHAN; and A SKETCH OF THE VILLAGE IN THE LAST CENTURY. 1 vol. 16mo. Cloth, 50 cents; cloth, gilt edge, 63 cents.

MRS. SARAH P. DOUGHTY. THE LITTLE CHILD'S FRIEND. With illustrations. 1 vol. square 16mo. Cloth, 38 cents.

MEMOIRS OF A LONDON DOLL. Written by herself. Edited by Mrs. Fairstair. With engravings. 1 vol. square 16mo. Scarlet cloth, 50 cents; gilt edge, 63 cents.

TALES FROM CATLAND, FOR LITTLE KITTENS. By an OLD TABBY. With engravings. 1 vol. square 16mo. Scarlet cloth, 50 cents; gilt edge, 63 cents.

THE DOLL AND HER FRIENDS; A Companion to the 'Memoirs of a London Doll.' With illustrations. 1 vol. square 16mo., 50 cents.

MRS. BARBAULD'S LESSONS FOR CHILDREN. With engravings. 16mo. Cloth, 40 cents.

JACOB ABBOTT'S JONAS'S STORIES. Related to ROLLO and LUCY. 18mo. Cloth, 38 cents.

JONAS A JUDGE ; or Law among the Boys. Cloth, 38 cents.

JONAS ON A FARM IN SUMMER. Cloth, 38 cents.

JONAS ON A FARM IN WINTER. Cloth, 38 cents.

The Same in two vols., red cloth, gilt, $1.50

JACK HALLIARD. VOYAGES AND ADVENTURES IN THE ARCTIC OCEAN. With Engravings. 16mo. Cloth, 38 cents.

S. G. GOODRICH'S

LAMBERT LILLY'S HISTORY OF THE NEW-ENGLAND STATES. With numerous Engravings. 18mo. Cloth, 38 cts.

LAMBERT LILLY'S HISTORY OF THE MIDDLE STATES. With numerous Engravings. 18mo. Cloth, 38 cents.

LAMBERT LILLY'S HISTORY OF THE SOUTHERN STATES : Virginia, North and South Carolina, and Georgia. With numerous Engravings. 18mo. Cloth, 38 cents.

LAMBERT LILLY'S HISTORY OF THE WESTERN STATES. With numerous Engravings. 18mo. Cloth, 38 cents.

LAMBERT LILLY'S STORY OF THE AMERICAN REVOLUTION. With numerous Engravings. 18mo. Cloth, 38 cents.

THE SAME, in 3 Vols. Red cloth, gilt, $1.88.

MARY HOWITT'S BIRDS AND FLOWERS, AND OTHER COUNTRY THINGS. With Engravings. 12mo. 50 cents.

PARLEY'S SHORT STORIES FOR LONG NIGHTS. With eight colored Engravings, 16mo. cloth, 50 cents ; uncolored Engravings, 40 cents.

PARLEY'S SMALL PICTURE BOOKS. With colored Frontispieces, printed covers. 16mo. Eight kinds, assorted. Per gross, $9.00.

THE DUCKS AND THE FROGS. With Engravings from Designs by BILLINGS. 13 cents.

THE INDESTRUCTIBLE BOOKS FOR CHILDREN. Printed on strong Cloth, expressly prepared. Four kinds, viz. : Alphabet — Primer — Spelling Book — Reading Book. Each 25 cents.

THE FOUR PARTS, Bound in one Cloth volume, 90 Pictures, $1.25.

R. C. Waterston.

THALATTA:

A

BOOK FOR THE SEA-SIDE.

'As soon as the men who were in the vanguard had climbed the hill and beheld the Sea, they gave a great shout, . . . crying out, "Thalatta! Thalatta!"'
Xenophon's Expedition of Cyrus, IV. 7.

BOSTON:
TICKNOR, REED, AND FIELDS.
MDCCCLIII.

THURSTON, TORRY, AND EMERSON, PRINTERS.

. . . . . . Leaves
Under which the bright sea heaves,
While each breathless interval
In their whisperings musical
The inspired soul supplies
With its own deep melodies.

SHELLEY.

. . . God's own profound
Was above me, and round me the mountains,
And under, the sea;
And within me, my heart, to bear witness
What was and shall be.

BROWNING.

How sweet it were . . . . .
To hear each other's whispered speech;
Eating the Lotos day by day,
To watch the crisping ripples on the beach,
And tender curving lines of creamy spray.
To lend our hearts and spirits wholly
To the influence of mild-minded melancholy
To muse and brood, and live again in memory.

TENNYSON.

. . . . . That hears all night
The plunging seas draw backward from the land
Their moon-led waters white.

TENNYSON.

And the great sea-waves below,
Pulse o' the midnight, beating slow.

WHITTIER.

CONTENTS.

THALATTA.

PRELUDE.

Come o'er the green hills to the sunny sea!
  The boundless sea that washeth many lands,
Where shells unknown to England, fair and free,
  Lie brightly scatter'd on the gleaming sands.
There, 'midst the hush of slumbering ocean's roar,
  We'll sit and watch the silver-tissued waves
Creep languidly along the basking shore,
  And kiss thy gentle feet, like Eastern slaves.

And we will take some volume of our choice,
  Full of a quiet poetry of thought,
And thou shalt read me, with thy plaintive voice,
  Lines which some gifted mind hath sweetly wrought;
And I will listen, gazing on thy face,
  (Pale as some cameo on the Italian shell!)
Or looking out across the far blue space,
  Where glancing sails to gentle breezes swell.

Come forth! The sun hath flung on Thetis' breast
  The glittering tresses of his golden hair;
All things are heavy with a noonday rest,
  And floating sea-birds leave the stirless air.

Against the sky, in outlines clear and rude,
  The cleft rocks stand, while sunbeams slant between;
And lulling winds are murmuring through the wood,
  Which skirts the bright bay with its fringe of green.

Come forth! All motion is so gentle now,
  It seems *thy* step alone should walk the earth,—
Thy voice alone, the 'ever soft and low,'
  Wake the far-haunting echoes into birth.
Too wild would be Love's passionate store of hope,
  Unmeet the influence of his changeful power,—
Ours be companionship, whose gentle scope
  Hath charm enough for such a tranquil hour.

And slowly, idly wandering, we will roam,
  Where the high cliffs shall give us ample shade;
And watch the glassy waves, whose wrathful foam
  Hath power to make the seaman's heart afraid.
Seek thou no veil to shroud thy soft brown hair,—
  Wrap thou no mantle round thy graceful form;
The cloudless sky smiles forth as still and fair,
  As though earth ne'er could know another storm.

Come! Let not listless sadness make delay,—
  Beneath Heaven's light that sadness will depart;
And as we wander on our shoreward way,
  A strange, sweet peace shall enter in thine heart.
We will not weep, nor talk of vanish'd years,
  When, link by link, Hope's glittering chain was riven:
Those who are dead, shall claim from love no tears,—
  Those who have injured us, shall be forgiven.

We will not mar the scene — we will not look
  To the veil'd future, or the shadowy past;
Seal'd up shall be sad Memory's open book,
  And childhood's idleness return at last!
Joy, with his restless, ever-fluttering wings,
  And hope, his gentle brother, — all shall cease:
Like weary hinds that seek the desert springs,
  Our one sole feeling shall be peace — deep peace!

Mrs. Norton.

4

THALATTA.

THALATTA! Thalatta!
I greet thee, thou Ocean eternal!
I give thee ten thousand times greeting,
With heart all exulting,
As, ages since, hailed thee
Those ten thousand Greek hearts
Fate-conquering, home-yearning,
World-renowned Greek hearts.

The billows were rolling,
Were rolling and roaring,
The sun poured downward incessant,
The flickering rose-lights;
Affrighted, the flocks of the sea-mews
Fluttered away, loud-screaming;
The steeds were stamping, the shields were
clanging,
And far, like a shout of victory, echoed
Thalatta! Thalatta!

Thou Ocean eternal, I greet thee!
Like the tongue of my home is the dash of thy waters!
Like dreams of my childhood now sparkle before me
All the wide curving waves of thy rolling dominions.

I hear, as told newly, the old recollections
Of the trifles I loved in the days of my boyhood.
Of the bright gifts that glittered at Christmas; —
Of the scarlet branches of coral,
Of the gold fish, the pearls and gay sea-shells,
Of all that thou guardest in secret
Below in thy houses of crystal!

Oh! how have I languished,
Aweary in exile!
Like a poor faded flower shut up in an herbal
Lay my heart in my bosom;
'T is as if I had sat through the winter
A sick man shut up in my chamber,
And now I had suddenly left it, —
And dazzlingly glitters upon me
The emerald Spring, sun-awakened!
On the trees are the white blossoms rustling,
And the young flowers look up unto me,
With moist loving eyes full of beauty.
All is fragrance and murmurs and soft airs and
laughter,
And in the blue heavens the birds are a-singing
Thalatta! Thalatta!

From the German of HEINE.

THE LIFE OF SEAS.

THESE grassy vales are warm and deep,
Where apple-orchards wave and glow;
Upon soft uplands whitening sheep
Drift in long wreaths. Below
Sun-fronting beds of garden-thyme, alive
With the small humming merchants of the hive;
And cottage homes in every shady nook
Where willows dip and kiss the dimples of the brook.

But all too close against my face
My thick breath feels these crowding trees;
They crush me in their green embrace:—
I miss the Life of Seas;
The wild free life that round the flinty shores
Of my bleak isles expanded ocean pours,—
So free, so far, that in the lull of even,
Nought but the rising moon stands in your path to heaven.

These inland love-bowers sweetly bloom,
White with the hawthorn's summer snows;
Along soft turf a purple bloom
The elm at sunset throws;

There the fond lover, listening for the sweet
Half soundless coming of his maiden's feet,
Thrills if the linnet's rustling pinions pass,
Or some light leaf is blown rippling along the grass.

But Love his pain as sweetly tells
Beneath some cavern beetling hoar,
Where silver sands and rosy shells
Pave the smooth, glistening shore, —
When all the winds are low, and to thy tender
Accents, the wavelets, stealing in, make slender
And tinkling cadence, wafting, every one
A golden smile to thee from the fast-sinking sun.

Or if (like some) thou 'st loved in vain,
Or madly wooed the already won, —
Go, when the Passion and the Pain
Their havoc have begun,
And dare the Thunder, rolling up behind
The Deep, to match that hurricane of mind;
Or to the sea-winds, raging on thy pale
Grief-wasted cheek, pour forth as bitter keen a tale.

For in that sleepless, tumbling tide, —
When most thy fevered spirits reel,
Sick with desires unsatisfied, —
Dwell life and balm to heal.
Raise thy free sail, and seek o'er ocean's breast —
It boots not what — those rose-clouds in the west,
And deem that thus thy spirit freed shall be,
Ploughing the stars through seas of blue eternity.

B. Simmons.

THE SPELL OF THE SEA.

I NEVER think without a thrill
Of wild and pure delight
Of all the leagues of blue, blue sea,
Which I have sailed o'er merrily
In day or dead of night.

With moon and stars, at morn and eve,
In sunny wind or shower,
How often hath it worked in me, —
That mystery of the kingly sea,
With joyous spells of power!

O it is well sick men should go
Unto the royal sea;
For on their souls, as on a glass,
From its bright fields the breath doth pass
Of its infinity.

My mother taught me how to love
The mystery of the sea;
She sported with my childish wonder
At its white waves and gentle thunder, —
Like a man's deep voice to me.

When in my soul dim thoughts awoke,
She helped to set them free;
I learned from ocean's murmurings
How infinite, eternal things,
Though viewless, yet could be.

In gentle moods I love the hills
Because they bound my spirit;
But to the broad blue sea I fly
When I would feel the destiny
Immortal souls inherit.

F. W. Faber.

O YE KEEN BREEZES.

O ye keen breezes from the salt Atlantic,
Which to the beach, where memory loves to wander,
On your strong pinions waft reviving coolness,
Bend your course hither!

For, in the surf ye scattered to the sunshine,
Did we not sport together in my boyhood,
Screaming for joy amid the flashing breakers,
O rude companions?

Then to the meadows beautiful and fragrant,
Where the coy Spring beholds her earliest verdure
Brighten with smiles that rugged sea-side hamlet,
How would we hasten!

There under elm-trees affluent in foliage,
High o'er whose summit hovered the sea-eagle,
Through the hot, glaring noontide have we rested
After our gambols.

Vainly the sailor called you from your slumber:
Like a glazed pavement shone the level ocean;
While, with the snow-white canvass idly drooping,
Stood the tall vessels.

And when, at length, exulting ye awakened,
Rushed to the beach, and ploughed the liquid acres,
How have I chased you through the shivered billows,
In my frail shallop!

Playmates, old playmates, hear my invocation!
In the close town I waste this golden summer,
Where piercing cries and sounds of wheels in motion
Ceaselessly mingle.

When shall I feel your breath upon my forehead?
When shall I hear you in the elm-trees' branches?
When shall we wrestle in the briny surges,
Friends of my boyhood?

EPES SARGENT.

11

WHERE IS THE SEA?

SONG OF THE GREEK ISLANDER IN EXILE.

[A Greek Islander, being taken to the Vale of Tempe, and called upon to admire its beauty, only replied — '*The sea — where is it?*']

WHERE is the sea? — I languish here —
  Where is my own blue sea?
With all its barks in fleet career,
  And flags, and breezes free.

I miss that voice of waves which first
  Awoke my childhood's glee;
The measured chime — the thundering burst —
  Where is my own blue sea?

Oh! rich your myrtle's breath may rise,
  Soft, soft your winds may be;
Yet my sick heart within me dies —
  Where is my own blue sea?

I hear the shepherd's mountain flute —
  I hear the whispering tree; —
The echoes of my soul are mute:
  — Where is my own blue sea?

MRS. HEMANS.

SALUTATION.

God be with thee, gladsome Ocean!
  How gladly greet I thee once more!
Ships, and waves, and ceaseless motion,
  And men rejoicing on thy shore.

Dissuading spake the mild physician,
  'Those briny waves for thee are death!'
But my soul fulfilled her mission,
  And lo! I breathe untroubled breath!

Fashion's pining sons and daughters
  Who seek the crowd they seem to fly,
Trembling they approach thy waters;
  And what cares Nature, if they die?

Me a thousand hopes and pleasures,
  A thousand recollections bland,
Thoughts sublime and stately measures,
  Revisit on thy echoing strand:

Dreams (the soul herself forsaking),
  Tearful raptures, boyish mirth;
Silent adorations, making
  A blessed shadow of this earth!

O ye hopes, that stir within me,
  Health comes with you from above!
God is with me, God is in me!
  I cannot die, if Life be Love.

Coleridge.

WHITE-CAPT WAVES.

White-capt waves far round the Ocean,
  Leaping in thanks or leaping in play,
All your bright faces, in happy commotion,
  Make glad matins this summer day.

The rosy light through the morning's portals
  Tinges your crests with an August hue;
Calling on us, thought-prisoned mortals,
  Thus to live in the moment too.

For, graceful creatures, you live by dying,
  Save your life, when you fling it away,
Flow through all forms, all form defying,
  And in wildest freedom strict rule obey.

Show us your art, O genial daughters
  Of solemn Ocean, thus to combine
Freedom and force of rolling waters
  With sharp observance of law divine.

J. F. Clarke.

SEA-VIEW FROM ST. LEONARD'S.

Hail to thy face and odors, glorious Sea!
'T were thanklessness in me to bless thee not,
Great beauteous Being! in whose breath and smile
My heart beats calmer, and my very mind
Inhales salubrious thoughts. How welcomer
Thy murmurs than the murmurs of the world!
Though like the world thou fluctuatest, thy din
To me is peace, thy restlessness repose.
Ev'n gladly I exchange yon spring-green lanes
With all the darling field-flowers in their prime,
And gardens haunted by the nightingale's
Long trills and gushing ecstacies of song,
For these wild headlands and the sea-mew's clang.

With thee beneath my windows, pleasant sea!
I long not to o'erlook earth's fairest glades
And green savannahs: Earth has not a plain
So boundless or so beautiful as thine.
The eagle's vision cannot take it in:
The lightning's wing, too weak to sweep its space,
Sinks half-way o'er it like a wearied bird:

It is the mirror of the stars, where all
Their hosts within the concave firmament,
Gay marching to the music of the spheres,
Can see themselves at once.

Nor on the stage
Of rural landscape are there lights and shades
Of more harmonious dance and play than thine.
How vividly this moment brightens forth,
Between gray parallel and leaden breadths,
A belt of hues that stripes thee many a league,
Flush'd like the rainbow, or the ring-dove's neck,
And giving to the glancing sea-bird's wing
The semblance of a meteor.

Mighty sea!
Cameleon-like thou changest, but there's love
In all thy change, and constant sympathy
With yonder sky — thy Mistress; from her brow
Thou tak'st thy moods, and wear'st her colors on
Thy faithful bosom; morning's milky white,
Noon's sapphire, or the saffron glow of eve;
And all thy balmier hours, fair Element!
Have such divine complexion — crisped smiles,
Luxuriant heavings, and sweet whisperings, —
That little is the wonder, Love's own Queen
From thee of old was fabled to have sprung. —
Creation's common! which no human power
Can parcel or enclose; the lordliest floods
And cataracts, that the tiny hands of man
Can tame, conduct, or bound, are drops of dew
To thee, that could'st subdue the Earth itself,

And brook'st commandment from the heavens alone
For marshalling thy waves.

Yet, potent sea!
How placidly thy moist lips speak ev'n now
Along yon sparkling shingles! Who can be
So fanciless, as to feel no gratitude
That power and grandeur can be so serene,
Soothing the home-bound navy's peaceful way,
And rocking ev'n the fisher's little bark
As gently as a mother rocks her child?

. . . .

Earth has her gorgeous towns; the earth-circling sea
Has spires and mansions more amusive still —
Men's volant homes, that measure liquid space
On wheel or wing. The chariot of the land,
With pain'd and panting steeds and clouds of dust,
Has no sight-gladdening motion like these fair
Careerers with the foam beneath their bows,
Whose streaming ensigns charm the waves by day,
Whose carols and whose watch-bells cheer the night,
Moor'd as they cast the shadows of their masts
In long array, or hither flit and yond
Mysteriously with slow and crossing lights,
Like spirits on the darkness of the deep.

There is a magnet-like attraction in
These waters to the imaginative power,
That links the viewless with the visible,
And pictures things unseen. To realms beyond
Yon highway of the world my fancy flies,
When by her tall and triple mast we know

Some nobler voyager, that has to woo
The trade-winds, and to stem the ecliptic surge.
The coral groves — the shores of conch and pearl,
Where she will cast her anchor, and reflect
Her cabin-window lights on warmer waves,
And under planets brighter than our own:
The nights of palmy isles, that she will see
Lit boundless by the fire-fly — all the smells
Of tropic fruits that will regale her — all
The pomp of nature, and the inspiriting
Varieties of life she has to greet, —
Come swarming o'er the meditative mind.

Campbell.

LINES WRITTEN AT SORRENTO.

The wild waves madly dash and roar,
  In thunder-throbs, upon the beach;
Their broad white hands upon the shore
  They struggle evermore to reach.

Up through the cavernous rocks amain,
  With short, hoarse growl, they plunge and leap,
Like an armed host, again and again,
  Battering some castellated steep.

Great pulses of the ocean heart,
  Beating from out immensity,
What mystic news would ye impart
  From the great spirit of the sea?

Ever, in still increasing force,
  Earnest as cries of love or hate,
Your large and eloquent discourse
  Is mighty as the march of fate.

I sit alone on the glowing sand,
  Filled with the music of your speech,
And only half may understand
  The wondrous lore that ye would teach.

The sea-weed and the shells are wise,
  And versed in your broad Sanscrit tongue;
The rocks need not our ears and eyes
  To comprehend the under-song.

The ocean and the shore are one;
  The rocks and trees that hang above,
The birds and insects in the sun
  Are linked in one strong tie of love.

Would that I might with freedom be
  A seer into your hidden truth,
Joining your firm fraternity,
  To drink with you perpetual youth!

C. P. Cranch.

HAMPTON BEACH.

The sunlight glitters keen and bright,
Where, miles away,
Lies stretching to my dazzled sight
A luminous belt, a misty light,
Beyond the dark pine bluffs and wastes of sandy grey.

The tremulous shadow of the sea!
Against its ground
Of silvery light, rock, hill, and tree,
Still as a picture, clear and free,
With varying outline mark the coast for miles around.

On — on — we tread with loose-flung rein
Our seaward way,
Through dark-green fields and blossoming grain,
Where the wild brier-rose skirts the lane,
And bends above our heads the flowering locust spray.

Ha! like a kind hand on my brow
Comes this fresh breeze,
Cooling its dull and feverish glow,
While through my being seems to flow
The breath of a new life — the healing of the seas!

Now rest we, where this grassy mound
His feet hath set
In the great waters, which have bound
His granite ankles greenly round
With long and tangled moss, and weeds with cool spray wet.

Good-bye to Pain and Care! I take
Mine ease to-day;
Here where these sunny waters break,
And ripples this keen breeze, I shake
All burdens from the heart, all weary thoughts away.

I draw a freer breath — I seem
Like all I see —
Waves in the sun — the white-winged gleam
Of sea-birds in the slanting beam —
And far-off sails which flit before the south wind free.

So when Time's veil shall fall asunder,
The soul may know
No fearful change, nor sudden wonder,
Nor sink the weight of mystery under,
But with the upward rise, and with the vastness grow.

And all we shrink from now may seem
No new revealing;
Familiar as our childhood's stream,
Or pleasant memory of a dream
The loved and cherished Past upon the new life stealing

Serene and mild the untried light
May have its dawning;
And, as in Summer's northern light
The evening and the dawn unite,
The sunset hues of Time blend with the soul's new morning.

I sit alone: in foam and spray
Wave after wave
Breaks on the rocks which, stern and grey,
Beneath like fallen Titans lay,
Or murmurs hoarse and strong through mossy cleft and cave.

What heed I of the dusty land
And noisy town?
I see the mighty deep expand
From its white line of glimmering sand
To where the blue of heaven on bluer waves shuts down!

In listless quietude of mind,
I yield to all
The change of cloud and wave and wind,
And passive on the flood reclined,
I wander with the waves, and with them rise and fall.

But look, thou dreamer! — wave and shore
In shadow lie;
The night-wind warns me back once more
To where my native hill-tops o'er
Bends like an arch of fire the glowing sunset sky!

So then, beach, bluff, and wave, farewell!
I bear with me
No token stone nor glittering shell,
But long and oft shall Memory tell
Of this brief thoughtful hour of musing by the sea.

J. G. Whittier.

THE SEA.

It keeps eternal whisperings around
Desolate shores, and with its mighty swell
Gluts twice ten thousand caverns, till the spell
Of Hecate leaves them their old shadowy sound.
Often 'tis in such gentle temper found,
That scarcely will the very smallest shell
Be moved for days from where it sometime fell,
When last the winds of heaven were unbound.
Oh, ye who have your eyeballs vexed and tired,
Feast them upon the wideness of the sea;
Oh, ye whose ears are dinned with uproar rude,
Or fed too much with cloying melody,
Sit ye near some old cavern's mouth, and brood
Until ye start, as if the sea-nymphs quired!

Keats.

APOSTROPHE TO THE OCEAN.

Roll on, thou deep and dark blue Ocean — roll!
Ten thousand fleets sweep over thee in vain;
Man marks the earth with ruin — his control
Stops with the shore; — upon the watery plain
The wrecks are all thy deed, nor doth remain
A shadow of man's ravage, save his own,
When, for a moment, like a drop of rain,
He sinks into thy depths with bubbling groan,
Without a grave, unknell'd, uncoffin'd, and unknown.

His steps are not upon thy paths, — thy fields
Are not a spoil for him, — thou dost arise
And shake him from thee; the vile strength he wields
For earth's destruction thou dost all despise,
Spurning him from thy bosom to the skies,
And send'st him, shivering in thy playful spray
And howling, to his Gods, where haply lies
His petty hope in some near port or bay,
And dashest him again to earth: — there let him lay.

The armaments which thunderstrike the walls
Of rock-built cities, bidding nations quake,
And monarchs tremble in their capitals,
The oak leviathans, whose huge ribs make

Their clay creator the vain title take
Of lord of thee, and arbiter of war:
These are thy toys, and, as the snowy flake,
They melt into thy yeast of waves, which mar
Alike the Armada's pride, or spoils of Trafalgar.

Thy shores are empires, changed in all save thee—
Assyria, Greece, Rome, Carthage, what are they?
Thy waters wasted them while they were free,
And many a tyrant since; their shores obey
The stranger, slave, or savage; their decay
Has dried up realms to deserts:—not so thou,
Unchangeable save to thy wild waves' play—
Time writes no wrinkle on thine azure brow—
Such as creation's dawn beheld, thou rollest now.

Thou glorious mirror, where the Almighty's form
Glasses itself in tempests; in all time,
Calm or convulsed—in breeze, or gale, or storm,
Icing the pole, or in the torrid clime
Dark-heaving;—boundless, endless, and sublime—
The image of Eternity—the throne
Of the Invisible; even from out thy slime
The monsters of the deep are made; each zone
Obeys thee; thou goest forth, dread, fathomless, alone.

And I have loved thee, Ocean! and my joy
Of youthful sports was on thy breast to be
Borne, like thy bubbles, onward: from a boy
I wanton'd with thy breakers—they to me

Were a delight; and if the freshening sea
Made them a terror—'twas a pleasing fear,
For I was as it were a child of thee,
And trusted to thy billows far and near,
And laid my hand upon thy mane—as I do here.

BYRON.

THE ocean looketh up to heaven,
As 'twere a living thing;
The homage of its waves is given,
In ceaseless worshipping.

They kneel upon the sloping sand
As bends the human knee,
A beautiful and tireless band,
The priesthood of the sea.

The sky is as a temple's arch,
The blue and wavy air
Is glorious with the spirit-march
Of messengers at prayer.

J. G. WHITTIER.

HYMN TO THE SEA.

Who shall declare the secret of thy birth,
Thou old companion of the circling earth?
And having reached with keen poetic sight
Ere beast or happy bird
Through the vast silence stirred,
Roll back the folded darkness of the primal night?

. . . .

Thou and the earth, twin sisters, as they say,
In the old prime were fashioned in one day;
And therefore thou delightest evermore
With her to lie and play
The summer hours away,
Curling thy loving ripples up her quiet shore.

She is a married matron long ago
With nations at her side; her milk doth flow
Each year; but thee no husband dares to tame,
Thy wild will is thine own,
Thy sole and virgin throne —
Thy mood is ever changing — thy resolve the same.

Sunlight and moonlight minister to thee;—
O'er the broad circles of the shoreless sea
Heaven's two great lights forever set and rise;
While the round vault above
In vast and silent love
Is gazing down upon thee with his hundred eyes.

All night thou utterest forth thy solemn moan,
Counting the weary minutes all alone;
Then in the morning thou dost calmly lie
Deep blue, ere yet the sun
His day-work hath begun
Under the opening windows of the golden sky.

The spirit of the mountain looks on thee
Over an hundred hills; quaint shadows flee
Across thy marbled mirror; brooding lie
Storm-mists of infant cloud
With a sight-baffling shroud,
Mantling the grey-blue islands in the western sky.

. . . .

Daughter and darling of remotest eld—
Time's childhood, and Time's age thou hast beheld;
His arm is feeble, and his eye is dim;
He tells old tales again,—
He wearies of long pain—
Thou art as at the first—thou journiedst not with him.

Henry Alford.

O HOLY SEA!

O CRADLE of the rising sun, O holy sea!
  O grave of every setting sun, O holy sea!
O thou in balmy nights outspreading the crystal mirror
  Where Luna looks, — a silent nun, — O holy sea!
O thou in silent midnights chiming, through thy wide
      realm,
  With starry choirs, — sweet unison, — O holy sea!
The morning's and the evening's red bloom out from
      thee,
  Two roses of thy garden-bed, O holy sea!
O Amphitrite's panting bosom, whose heavy waves
  Now swell, now sink, beneath the moon, O holy sea!
O Aphrodite's womb maternal! bring forth thy child,
  And borrow splendor from thy son, O holy sea!
Sprinkle the earth's green wreath of spring with pearly
      dew,
  For thine the pearls are, every one, O holy sea!
The Naiads of the meadows all, that sprang from thee,
  Come back as Nereids at thy call, O holy sea!
The ships of thought sail over thee and sink in thee;
  Atlantis rests there, mighty one, O holy sea!
The beaker of the gods, that fell from high Olympus,
  Hangs on the coral-twigs, far down, O holy sea!
My spirit yearneth like the moon to sink in thee;
  Forth send me from thee like the sun, O holy sea!

From the German of RÜCKERT.

HYMN TO THE SEA.

Along yon soft tumultuousness, the dawn
Reaches a glowing hand, and the mute world
Thrills back to life. This lustrous blossom, curled
In on its dreaming heart, feels the forlorn
Old Shadow lift, and guardedly discloses
Its wayside cheer; and endless waves away
Flash the broad triumph of the light,
Rejoicing in the infinite
And quenchless possibility of Day;
Day,—that at least shall win far more than darkness loses.

Over those morning waves, or when the bare
Stars glow, or moon her tireless lover nears,
The eternal Beauty, that, these countless years,
Makes earthly musings so divinely fair,
Broods, listening to the prophecy thou chantest;—
The subtle breath of mortal sympathies
Is she — wooing us unto right
In unsuspected ways — a light
From inmost heaven, tempered to dreaming eyes—
A sweet foreshadow of the joy for which thou pantest.

Roll in from far thy deep, broad-skirted thunder,
On which the wild winds fawn! *Thy* voice by day!
But night adopts and trances it away
Into its clear, sad universe of wonder.
O, weary of life's shallow, lavish sound,
Enrich me beyond hunger with that tone!
Tell in what deep, grey solitude
Thy voice is born — what caverns rude
Still haunt it — and if the Infinite ALONE
Touch it himself with calm, and utterance so profound.

I am borne outward by this fragrant breeze,
Which seems to press its warm lips to the sand
And then away, — beyond the singing land,
To that hoar silence of the lone mid-seas,
Where thou, in unrelated strength, a bare,
Vast heart, throbbest beneath the eternal Eye.
Life soars like an enfranchised flame;
The needy doubt, the hope, that came
Before the laggard dawn to wake me, — fly;
And dim Eternity flows in, like silent air.

Do tempests swing thee, or deep, choral nights
Chant unto murmurous slumber — yield me still
The calm of hushed abysses: human ill,
Patience transfigures on her visioned heights.
Thou dost not rive the blood-drenched deck apart,
Nor whelm the slaver's freight of woes; but, soft,
On patient, swelling breast upborne,
Waftest the dismal burthen on,
As trusting in the love that waits aloft,
And the slow germ of good in man's unquiet heart.

Ah! meagre happiness! and hopes that reach
To some dull dream, a vapor of the sense —
And, on the plain of the old Permanence,
Are but as hasty sunshine in the beach
Of idle footprints! O make more divine
Dim sea, our thoughts! nor may we dully grope
Mid slavish fears, while thou dost girth
All continents and isles with mirth,
And music of unconquerable hope
That Light and Freedom shall be earth's, as they are thine.

Oh, old Consoler! that dost tenderly
In thy great longing merge my day-born pain,
Uplift me to the stature of your strain,
And bid all vulgar aspirations flee!
The nobler earth is built of stubborn good;
Who brings his little vanity, his grave
Appeal to men's applause or wonder,
Warn him away with thy deep thunder!
Flash o'er the graven sands a liberal wave
And let us know no more his memory or his blood!

Mild, herald beams, wooing the folded sight,
Shed warmth far down in many a sunless nook.
Thank God, there are no eyes in which we look,
But some heart's love doth lend them beauteous light!
Dreams that prefigure hopes, and hopes that take
Fresh courage from all life — from starlight bold,
Sung softly in by whippoorwills —
From sunset's broad'ning sails, o'er hills
Afar — and from the earth that grows not old, —
Float lightly o'er our heads, whether we sleep or wake.

Alas! to her high place, through sea-deep tears,
Earth wins her long, slow, agonizing way;
The base, triumphant despot of a day
Is weary Anarch of a thousand years.
And yet this many a spring the boughs are sheen
With the almost forgotten bloom. Call, Sea,
Unto all faithful souls, Doubt not,
Aspire to lead earth's struggling thought
Still up;—bring what from full hearts gushes free;
He, who doth blend and shape the whole, finds nothing mean.

When morning, loosing from its crimson drifts,
O'ertakes some panting melody, most tender
Of such weak rivalship, and prone to render
Homage unto great-heartedness,—it lifts
The breaking strain, and all along its lines
Of thrilling light, its currents of pure air
And rosy mists, winds it at will—
Unites and separates, and still
Wreathes it and builds anew beyond despair;
Till song is light—light, song—through all heaven's steadfast signs.

O know how all things change! Night's violet star
Erewhile bloomed red; and thou, Sea, wear'st away
The glorious realm of a forgotten day,
But lay'st the pillars of a fairer far,
Deep in thy caverned bed. For all that ever
Gathered about it men's delight or love,
Or aught that simply blooms or strives
To make more beautiful our lives,
In each new fabric of the world, is wove
Afresh, and changes like the light, but passes never.

ANNE WHITNEY.

THE SOUND OF THE SEA.

Thou art sounding on, thou mighty sea,
For ever and the same!
The ancient rocks yet ring to thee,
Whose thunders nought can tame.

Oh! many a glorious voice is gone,
From the rich bowers of earth,
And hush'd is many a lovely one
Of mournfulness or mirth.

The Dorian flute that sighed of yore
Along thy wave, is still;
The harp of Judah peals no more
On Zion's awful hill.

And Memnon's lyre hath lost the chord
That breath'd the mystic tone,
And the songs, at Rome's high triumphs pour'd,
Are with her eagles flown.

And mute the Moorish horn, that rang
  O'er stream and mountain free,
And the hymn the leagued Crusaders sang,
  Hath died in Galilee.

But thou art swelling on, thou deep,
  Through many an olden clime,
Thy billowy anthem, ne'er to sleep
  Until the close of time.

Thou liftest up thy solemn voice
  To every wind and sky,
And all our earth's green shores rejoice
  In that one harmony.

It fills the noontide's calm profound,
  The sunset's heaven of gold;
And the still midnight hears the sound,
  Even as when first it roll'd.

Let there be silence deep and strange,
  Where sceptred cities rose!
Thou speak'st of One who doth not change —
  — So may our hearts repose.

MRS. HEMANS.

HYMN OF THE SEA.

The sea is mighty, but a Mightier sways
His restless billows. Thou, whose hands have scooped
His boundless gulfs and built his shore, thy breath
That moved in the beginning o'er his face
Moves o'er it evermore. The obedient waves
To its strong motion roll, and rise and fall.
Still from that realm of rain a cloud goes up,
As at the first, to water the great earth,
And keep her valleys green. A hundred realms
Watch its broad shadow warping on the wind,
And in the dropping shower, with gladness hear
Thy promise of the harvest. I look forth
Over the boundless blue, where joyously
The bright crests of innumerable waves
Glance to the sun at once, as when the hands
Of a great multitude are upward flung
In acclamation. I behold the ships
Gliding from cape to cape, from isle to isle,
Or stemming towards far lands, or hastening home
From the old world. It is thy friendly breeze
That bears them, with the riches of the land,

And treasure of dear lives, till in the port
The shouting seaman climbs and furls the sail.

But who shall bide thy tempest, who shall face
The blast that wakes the fury of the sea?
O God! thy justice makes the world turn pale,
When on the armed fleet, that royally
Bears down the surges, carrying war, to smite
Some city, or invade some thoughtless realm,
Descends the fierce tornado. The vast hulks
Are whirled like chaff upon the waves; the sails
Fly, rent like webs of gossamer; the masts
Are snapped asunder; downward from the decks,
Downward are slung, into the fathomless gulf,
Their cruel engines; and their hosts, arrayed
In trappings of the battle-field, are whelmed
By whirlpools, or dashed dead upon the rocks.
Then stand the nations still with awe, and pause,
A moment, from the bloody work of war.

These restless surges eat away the shores
Of earth's old continents; the fertile plain
Welters in shallows, headlands crumble down,
And the tide drifts the sea-sand in the streets
Of the drowned city. Thou, meanwhile, afar
In the green chambers of the middle sea,
Where broadest spread the waters and the line
Sinks deepest, while no eye beholds thy work,
Creator! thou dost teach the coral worm
To lay his mighty reefs. From age to age
He builds beneath the waters till at last

His bulwarks overtop the brine, and check
The long wave rolling from the southern pole
To break upon Japan. Thou bidst the fires
That smoulder under ocean, heave on high
The new-made mountains, and uplift their peaks,
A place of refuge for the storm-driven bird.
The birds and wafting billows plant the rifts
With herb and tree; sweet fountains gush; sweet airs
Ripple the living lakes that, fringed with flowers,
Are gathered in the hollows. Thou dost look
On thy creation and pronounce it good.
Its valleys, glorious with their summer green,
Praise thee in silent beauty, and its woods,
Swept by the murmuring winds of ocean, join
The murmuring shores in a perpetual hymn.

W. C. Bryant.

SONNET.

THE ocean, at the bidding of the moon,
Forever changes with his restless tide;
Flung shoreward now, to be re-gather'd soon
With kingly pauses of reluctant pride
And semblance of return: — Anon from home
He issues forth anew, high-ridged and free —
The gentlest murmur of his seething foam,
Like armies whispering where great echoes be!
Oh leave me here upon this beach to rove,
Mute listener to that sound, so grand and lone —
A glorious sound, deep drawn and strongly thrown,
And reaching those on mountain-heights above,
To British ears (as who shall scorn to own?)
A tutelar fond voice, a saviour-tone of love!

CHARLES TENNYSON.

COUNT ARNALDOS.

Who had ever such adventure,
Holy priest or virgin nun,
As befel the Count Arnaldos
At the rising of the sun?

On his wrist the hawk was hooded,
Forth with horn and hound went he,
When he saw a stately galley
Sailing on the silent sea.

Sail of satin, mast of cedar,
Burnished poop of beaten gold, —
Many a morn you'll hood your falcon,
Ere you such a bark behold.

Sails of satin, masts of cedar,
Golden poops may come again,
But mortal ear no more shall listen
To yon grey-haired sailor's strain.

Heart may beat, and eye may glisten,
  Faith is strong, and Hope is free,
But mortal ear no more shall listen
  To the song that rules the sea.

When the grey-haired sailor chaunted,
  Every wind was hushed to sleep, —
Like a virgin's bosom panted
  All the wide reposing deep.

Bright in beauty rose the star-fish
  From her green cave down below,
Right above the eagle poised him —
  Holy music charmed them so.

'Stately galley! glorious galley!
  God hath poured his grace on thee!
Thou alone mayst scorn the perils
  Of the dread devouring sea!

'False Almeria's reefs and shallows,
  Black Gibraltar's giant rocks,
Sound and sand-bank, gulf and whirlpool,
  All, my glorious galley mocks!'

'For the sake of God our Maker!'
  (Count Arnaldos' cry was strong) —
'Old man, let me be partaker
  In the secret of thy song!'

'Count Arnaldos! Count Arnaldos!
  Hearts I read, and thoughts I know;—
Wouldst thou learn the ocean secret,
  In our galley thou must go.'

From the Spanish.

TREASURES OF THE DEEP.

What hid'st thou in thy treasure-caves and cells,
  Thou hollow-sounding and mysterious Main?
Pale glist'ning pearls, and rainbow-colored shells,
  Bright things which gleam unreck'd of, and in vain.
Keep, keep thy riches, melancholy sea!
    We ask not such from thee.

Yet more, the Depths have more!—What wealth untold,
  Far down, and shining through their stillness, lies!
Thou hast the starry gems, the burning gold,
  Won from ten thousand royal Argosies.
Sweep o'er thy spoils, thou wild and wrathful Main!
    Earth claims not these again!

Yet more, the Depths have more! — Thy waves have
roll'd
Above the cities of the world gone by!
Sand hath filled up the palaces of old,
Seaweed o'ergrown the halls of revelry!
Dash o'er them Ocean! in thy scornful play,
Man yields them to decay!

Yet more! the Billows and the Depths have more!
High hearts and brave are gathered to thy breast!
They hear not now the booming waters roar, —
The battle-thunders will not break their rest.
Keep thy red gold and gems, thou stormy grave! —
Give back the true and brave!

Give back the lost and lovely! — Those for whom
The place was kept at board and hearth so long,
The prayer went up through midnight's breathless
gloom,
And the vain yearning woke 'midst festal song!
Hold fast thy buried isles, thy towers o'erthrown,
— But all is not thine own!

To thee the love of woman hath gone down,
Dark flow thy tides o'er manhood's noble head,
O'er youth's bright locks and beauty's flowery crown;
Yet must thou hear a voice — Restore the dead!
Earth shall reclaim her precious things from thee;
Restore the dead, thou Sea!

Mrs. Hemans.

THE LITTLE BEACH-BIRD.

I.

Thou little bird, thou dweller by the sea,
  Why takest thou its melancholy voice?
    And with that boding cry
    Along the waves dost thou fly?
O! rather, Bird, with me
  Through the fair land rejoice!

II.

Thy flitting form comes ghostly, dim, and pale,
  As driven by a beating storm at sea;
    Thy cry is weak and scared,
    As if thy mates had shared
The doom of us. Thy wail —
  What does it bring to me?

III.

Thou call'st along the sand, and haunt'st the surge,
  Restless and sad; as if in strange accord
    With the motion and the roar
    Of waves that drive to shore,
One spirit did ye urge —
  The Mystery — The Word.

IV.

Of thousands, thou, both sepulchre and pall,
  Old Ocean, art! A requiem o'er the dead,
    From out thy gloomy cells
    A tale of mourning tells —
Tells of man's woe and fall,
  His sinless glory fled.

V.

Then turn thee, little bird, and take thy flight
  Where the complaining sea shall sadness bring
    Thy spirit never more.
    Come, quit with me the shore,
For gladness and the light
  Where birds of summer sing.

R. H. Dana.

THE LEE-SHORE.

Sleet, and Hail, and Thunder!
  And ye Winds that rave
Till the sands thereunder
  Tinge the sullen wave —

Winds that like a demon
  Howl with horrid note
Round the toiling seaman
  In his tossing boat —

From his humble dwelling
  On the shingly shore,
Where the billows swelling
  Keep such hollow roar —

From that weeping woman
  Seeking with her cries
Succor superhuman
  From the frowning skies —

From the urchin pining
  For his father's knee —
From the lattice shining —
  Drive him out to sea!

Let broad leagues dissever
  Him from yonder foam; —
O God! to think man ever
  Comes too near his Home!

THOMAS HOOD.

THE OCEAN'S MOAN.

πᾶσαν δ' ἐπλησας φωνας ἅλα. MOSCHUS.

STREAMS that sweep where thousands languish
On the mountain, in the glen,
Seaward bear each cry of anguish
Uttered by the sons of men;

Hence it is that ever Ocean
Hath so sad, so wild a moan;
Calm, or lashed in wild commotion,
Therefore is its dirge-like tone.

Moaning for the dead and dying
With its ever voiceful waves,
For the countless forms that lying
Whiten in its coral caves;
Earth the broken-hearted pillows,
Rivers tell it to the sea,
Shall not Ocean, with its billows,
Their eternal mourner be?

ANONYMOUS.

THE WRECK OF THE HESPERUS.

It was the schooner Hesperus,
That sailed the wintry sea;
And the skipper had taken his little daughtér,
To bear him company.

Blue were her eyes as the fairy-flax,
Her cheeks like the dawn of day,
And her bosom white as the hawthorn buds,
That ope in the month of May.

The skipper he stood beside the helm
With his pipe in his mouth,
And watched how the veering flaw did blow
The smoke now West, now South.

Then up and spoke an old sailór,
Had sailed the Spanish Main,
'I pray thee, put into yonder port,
For I fear a hurricane.

'Last night, the moon had a golden ring,
And to-night no moon we see!'
The skipper, he blew a whiff from his pipe,
And a scornful laugh laughed he.

Colder and louder blew the wind,
A gale from the north-east;
The snow fell hissing in the brine,
And the billows frothed like yeast.

Down came the storm, and smote amain,
The vessel in its strength;
She shuddered and paused like a frighted steed,
Then leaped her cable's length.

'Come hither! come hither! my little daughtér,
And do not tremble so;
For I can weather the roughest gale,
That ever wind did blow.'

He wrapped her warm in his seaman's coat
Against the stinging blast;
He cut a rope from a broken spar,
And bound her to the mast.

'O father! I hear the church-bells ring
O say, what may it be?'
''T is a fog-bell on a rock-bound coast!'—
And he steered for the open sea.

'O father! I hear the sound of guns,
O say, what may it be?'
'Some ship in distress, that cannot live
In such an angry sea!'

'O father! I see a gleaming light,
O say, what may it be?'
But the father answered never a word,
A frozen corpse was he.

Lashed to the helm, all stiff and stark,
With his face to the skies,
The lantern gleamed through the gleaming snow
On his fixed and glassy eyes.

Then the maiden clasped her hands and prayed
That savéd she might be;
And she thought of Christ, who stilled the wave,
On the Lake of Galilee.

And fast through the midnight dark and drear,
Through the whistling sleet and snow,
Like a sheeted ghost, the vessel swept
Towards the reef of Norman's Woe.

And ever the fitful gusts between
A sound came from the land;
It was the sound of the trampling surf,
On the rocks and the hard sea-sand.

4

The breakers were right beneath her bows,
 She drifted a dreary wreck,
And a whooping billow swept the crew
 Like icicles from her deck.

She struck where the white and fleecy waves
 Looked soft as carded wool,
But the cruel rocks, they gored her side
 Like the horns of an angry bull.

Her rattling shrouds, all sheathed in ice,
 With the masts went by the board;
Like a vessel of glass, she strove and sank,
 Ho! ho! the breakers roared!

At daybreak, on the bleak sea-beach,
 A fisherman stood aghast,
To see the form of a maiden fair,
 Lashed close to a drifting mast.

The salt sea was frozen on her breast,
 The salt tears in her eyes;
And he saw her hair, like the brown sea-weed,
 On the billows fall and rise.

Such was the wreck of the Hesperus,
 In the midnight and the snow!
Christ save us all from a death like this,
 On the reef of Norman's Woe!

H. W. Longfellow.

THE FUGITIVES.

I.

The waters are flashing,
The white hail is dashing,
The lightnings are glancing,
The hoar-spray is dancing—
Away!

The whirlwind is rolling,
The thunder is tolling,
The forest is swinging,
The minster bells ringing—
Come away!

The Earth is like Ocean,
Wreck-strewn and in motion:
Bird, beast, man, and worm,
Have crept out of the storm—
Come away!

II.

'Our boat has one sail,
And the helmsman is pale;—
A bold pilot I trow,
Who should follow us now,'—
Shouted he—

And she cried: 'Ply the oar;
Put off gaily from shore!' —
As she spoke, bolts of death
Mixed with hail, specked their path
O'er the sea.

And from isle, tower, and rock,
The blue beacon-cloud broke,
Though dumb in the blast,
The red cannon flashed fast
From the lee.

III.

'And fear'st thou, and fear'st thou?
And see'st thou, and hear'st thou?
And drive we not free
O'er the terrible sea,
I and thou?'

One boat-cloak did cover
The loved and the lover —
Their blood beats one measure,
They murmur proud pleasure
Soft and low; —

While around the lashed Ocean,
Like mountains in motion,
Is withdrawn and uplifted,
Sunk, shattered, and shifted,
To and fro.

IV.

In the court of the fortress
Beside the pale portress,
Like a blood-hound well beaten
The bridegroom stands, eaten
  By shame;

On the topmost watch-turret,
As a death-boding spirit,
Stands the grey tyrant father,
To his voice the mad weather
  Seems tame;

And with curses as wild
As e'er clung to child,
He devotes to the blast
The best, loveliest, and last
  Of his name!

SHELLEY.

SONG.

'O MARY, go and call the cattle home,
    And call the cattle home,
    And call the cattle home,
  Across the sands o' Dee;'
The western wind was wild and dank wi' foam,
  And all alone went she.

The creeping tide came up along the sand,
And o'er and o'er the sand,
And round and round the sand,
As far as eye could see;
The blinding mist came down and hid the land,—
And never home came she.

'O is it weed or fish or floating hair,
A tress o' golden hair,
O' drowned maiden's hair,
Above the nets at sea?
Was never salmon yet that shone so fair,
Among the stakes on Dee.'

They rowed her in across the rolling foam,
The cruel crawling foam,
The cruel hungry foam,
To her grave beside the sea;
But still the boatmen hear her call the cattle home
Across the sands o' Dee.

CHARLES KINGSLEY.

THE FISHERMAN.

A PERILOUS life, and sad as life may be,
Hath the lone fisher on the lonely sea,
O'er the wide waters laboring, far from home,
For some bleak pittance e'er compelled to roam;
Few hearts to cheer him through his dangerous life,
And none to aid him in the stormy strife;
Companion of the sea and silent air,
The lonely fisher thus must ever fare;
Without the comfort, hope, — with scarce a friend,
He looks through life, and only sees — its end!

BARRY CORNWALL.

SIR PATRICK SPENS.

THE king sits in Dunfermline town,
Drinking the blude-red wine;
'O where will I get a gude skipper,
To sail this new ship of mine?'

Then up and spake an eldern knight,
  Sat at the king's right knee, —
'Sir Patrick Spens is the best sailor,
  That ever sailed the sea.'

The king has written a braid letter
  And sealed it with his hand,
And sent it to Sir Patrick Spens,
  Was walking to the strand.

'To Noroway, to Noroway,
  To Noroway over the faem;
The king's daughter of Noroway,
  'T is thou must bring her hame.'

The first word that Sir Patrick read,
  Sae loud, loud, laughed he;
The next word that Sir Patrick read,
  The salt tear blinded his e'e.

'O wha is this has done this deed,
  And told the king o' me,
To send us out at this time o' the year,
  To sail upon the sea?

'Be it wind, be it weet, be it sail, be it sleet,
  Our ship must sail the faem;
The king's daughter of Noroway,
  'T is we must fetch her hame.'

They hoisted their sails on Monenday morn,
  Wi' a' the speed they may,
And they hae landed in Noroway
  Upon a Wodensday.

They hadna been a week, a week,
  In Noroway, but twae,
When that the lords o' Noroway
  Began aloud to say;

'Ye Scottishmen spend a' our king's gowd,
  And a' our queenis fee.'
'Ye lie, ye lie, ye liars loud!
  Fu' loud I hear ye lie!

'For I hae brought as much white monie
  As gane my men and me,
And I brought a half-fou o' gude red gowd,
  Out o'er the sea wi' me.

'Make ready, make ready, my merry men a'!
  Our gude ship sails the morn,'
'Now ever alake, my master dear,
  I fear a deadly storm.

'I saw the new moon, late yestreen,
  Wi' the auld moon in her arm;
And if we gang to sea, master,
  I fear we'll come to harm.'

They hadna sailed a league, a league,
  A league but barely three,
When the lift grew dark and the wind blew loud,
  And gurly grew the sea.

The ankers brak, and the topmasts lap,
  It was sic a deadly storm;
And the waves cam o'er the broken ship
  Till a' her sides were torn.

'O where will I get a gude sailor,
  To tak my helm in hand,
Till I get up to the tall topmast,
  To see if I can spy land?'

'O here am I, a sailor gude,
  To tak the helm in hand,
Till you go up to the tall topmast,
  But I fear you'll ne'er spy land.'

He hadna gane a step, a step,
  A step but barely ane,
When a bolt flew out of our goodly ship,
  And the salt sea it came in.

'Gae fetch a web o' the silken claith,
  Another o' the twine,
And wap them into our ship's side,
  And let na the sea come in.'

They fetched a web o' the silken claith,
  Another o' the twine,
And they wapped them round that gude ship's side,
  But still the sea came in.

O laith, laith, were our gude Scots lords
  To wet their cork-heeled shoon!
But lang or a' the play was played
  They wat their hats aboon.

And mony was the feather-bed,
  That floated on the faem;
And mony was the gude lord's son,
  That never mair cam hame.

The ladyes wrang their fingers white,
  The maidens tore their hair,
A' for the sake o' their true loves;
  For them they'll see nae mair.

O lang, lang, may the ladyes sit,
  Wi' their fans into their hand,
Before they see Sir Patrick Spens
  Come sailing to the strand!

And lang, lang, may the maidens sit,
  Wi' their gowd kames in their hair,
A' waiting for their ain dear loves!
  For them they 'll see nae mair.

O forty miles off Aberdeen,
'T is fifty fathoms deep,
And there lies gude Sir Patrick Spens,
Wi' the Scots lords at his feet.

Scottish Border Minstrelsy.

I STOOD upon the sullen shore,
And marked the waves, with wild unrest,
And with a deep continuous roar,
Break onward to their mother's breast.

But no glad greeting waited there
The sighing wanderers of the sea,
No grassy lawn or flowerets gay,
But sterile sand's dull vacancy.

Wailing with upborne cry they haste
As if relief, redress to find;
But on cold stones their passion waste,
Then back recoil, and die resigned.

ANONYMOUS.

APPLEDORE.

How looks Appledore in a storm?
  I have seen it when its crags seemed frantic,
  Butting against the maddened Atlantic,
When surge after surge would heap enorme
  Cliffs of emerald topped with snow,
  That lifted and lifted, and then let go
A great white avalanche of thunder,
  A grinding, blinding, deafening ire
Monadnock might have trembled under;
  And the island, whose rock-roots pierce below
  To where they are warmed with the central fire,
You could feel its granite fibres racked
  As it seemed to plunge with a shudder and thrill
  Right at the breast of the swooping hill,
And to rise again, snorting a cataract
Of rage-froth from every cranny and ledge,
  While the sea drew its breath in hoarse and deep,
And the next vast breaker curled its edge,
  Gathering itself for a mightier leap.

North, east, and south, there are reefs and breakers
  You would never dream of in smooth weather,
That toss and gore the sea for acres,
  Bellowing, and gnashing, and snarling together;

Look northward, where Duck Island lies,
And over its crown you will see arise,
Against a back-ground of slaty skies,
  A row of pillars still and white,
  That glimmer and then are out of sight,
As if the moon should suddenly kiss
  While you crossed the gusty desert by night,
The long colonnades of Persepolis,
And then as sudden a darkness should follow
To gulp the whole scene at a single swallow,
The city's ghost, the drear, brown waste,
And the string of camels, clumsy-paced: —
Look southward for White Island light,
  The lantern stands ninety feet o'er the tide;
There is first a half-mile of tumult and fight,
Of dash and roar, and tumble and fright,
  And surging bewilderment wild and wide,
Where the breakers struggle left and right,
  Then a mile or more of rushing sea,
And then the light-house slim and lone;
And whenever the whole weight of ocean is thrown
Full and fair on White Island head,
  A great mist-jötun you will see
  Lifting himself up silently
High and huge o'er the light-house top,
With hands of wavering spray outspread,
  Groping after the little tower
  That seems to shrink and shorten and cower,
Till the monster's arms of a sudden drop,
    And silently and fruitlessly
    He sinks again into the sea.

You, meanwhile, where drenched you stand,
  Awaken once more to the rush and roar,
And on the rock-point tighten your hand,
As you turn and see a valley deep,
  That was not there a moment before,
Suck rattling down between you and a heap
  Of toppling billow, whose instant fall
  Must sink the whole island once for all —
Or watch the silenter, stealthier seas
  Feeling their way to you more and more;
If they once should clutch you high as the knees,
They would hurl you down like a sprig of kelp,
Beyond all reach of hope or help; —
  And such in a storm is Appledore.

J. R. Lowell.

EBB-TIDE.

  The tide has ebbed away;
No more wild surgings 'gainst the adamant rocks,
No swayings of the sea-weed false that mocks
  The hues of gardens gay;
  No laugh of little wavelets at their play;
No lucid pools reflecting Heaven's brow —
Both storm and calm alike are ended now.

The bare grey rocks sit lone;
The shifting sand lies so smooth and dry
That not a wave might ever have swept by
To vex it with loud moan;
Only some weedy fragment blackening thrown
To rot beneath the sky, tells what has been,
But Desolation's self has grown serene.

Afar the mountains rise,
And the broad estuary widens out,
All sunshine; wheeling round and round about,
Seaward, a white bird flies;
A bird? Nay, seems it rather in these eyes
An angel; o'er Eternity's dim sea,
Beck'ning—'Come thou where all we glad souls be.'

O life! O silent shore,
Where we sit patient! O great sea beyond,
To which we look with solemn hope and fond,
But sorrowful no more!—
Would we were disembodied souls to soar,
And like white sea-birds wing the Infinite Deep!—
Till then, Thou, Just One! wilt our spirits keep.

Anonymous.

THE FISHER.

THE water rolled — the water swelled,
  A fisher sat thereby;
Cool to his very heart he watched
  His line with dreamy eye:
And while his dreamy watch he keeps
  The parted waves unclose,
And forth from out the ocean deeps
  A water maiden rose.

She sang to him, she spake to him, —
  'My brood why lurest thou,
With human wit and human craft,
  Up to the deadly glow?
Ah! couldst thou know, how well below
  Our peaceful lives are passed,
Thou'dst leave thine earth and plunge beneath,
  And breathe free health at last.

'Bathes not the golden sun his face —
  The moon too in the sea;
And rise they not from their resting-place
  More beautiful to see?

And lures thee not the clear deep heaven
  Within the waters blue —
And thy form so fair, so mirrored there
  In that eternal dew!'

The water rolled — the water swelled,
  It reached his naked feet;
He felt, as at his love's approach,
  His bounding bosom beat;
She spake to him, she sang to him,
  His short suspense is o'er;
Half drew she him, half dropped he in,
  And sank to rise no more.

From the German of GOETHE.

THE SYRENS.

THE sea is lonely, the sea is dreary,
The sea is restless and uneasy;
Thou seekest quiet, thou art weary,
Wandering thou knowest not whither; —
Our little isle is green and breezy,
Come and rest thee! O, come hither!
Come to this peaceful home of ours,
    Where evermore
The low west wind creeps panting up the shore
To be at rest among the flowers;

Full of rest, the green moss lifts,
   As the dark waves of the sea
Draw in and out of rocky rifts,
   Calling solemnly to thee
With voices deep and hollow; —
         'To the shore
      Follow! O, follow!
To be at rest for evermore!
         For evermore!'

   Look how the grey, old Ocean
From the depth of his heart rejoices,
Heaving with a gentle motion,
When he hears our restful voices;
List how he sings in an undertone,
Chiming with our melody;
And all sweet sounds of earth and air
Melt into one low voice alone,
That murmurs over the weary sea,
And seems to sing from everywhere, —
'Here mayest thou harbor peacefully,
Here mayest thou rest from the aching oar;
   Turn thy curvéd prow ashore,
And in our green isle rest for evermore!
         For evermore!'
And Echo half wakes in the wooded hill,
   And, to her heart so calm and deep,
   Murmurs over in her sleep,
Doubtfully pausing and murmuring still,
         'Evermore!'
            Thus, on Life's weary sea,
            Heareth the marinere

Voices sweet, from far and near,
Ever singing low and clear,
Ever singing longingly.

Is it not better here to be,
Than to be toiling late and soon?
In the dreary night to see
Nothing but the blood-red moon
Go up and down into the sea;
Or, in the loneliness of day,
To see the still seals only
Solemnly lift their faces grey,
Making it yet more lonely?
Is it not better, than to hear
Only the sliding of the wave
Beneath the plank, and feel so near
A cold and lonely grave,
A restless grave, where thou shalt lie
Even in death unquietly?
Look down beneath thy wave-worn bark,
Lean over the side and see
The leaden eye of the sidelong shark
Upturned patiently,
Ever waiting there for thee:
Look down and see those shapeless forms,
Which ever keep their dreamless sleep
Far down within the gloomy deep,
And only stir themselves in storms,
Rising like islands from beneath,
And snorting through the angry spray,
As the frail vessel perisheth
In the whirls of their unwieldy play;

Look down! Look down!
Upon the sea-weed, slimy and dark,
That waves its arms so lank and brown,
Beckoning for thee!
Look down beneath thy wave-torn bark
Into the cold depth of the sea!
Look down! Look down!
Thus, on Life's lonely sea,
Heareth the marinere
Voices sad, from far and near,
Ever singing full of fear,
Ever singing drearfully.

Here all is pleasant as a dream;
The wind scarce shaketh down the dew,
The green grass floweth like a stream
Into the ocean's blue;
Listen! O, listen!
Here is a gush of many streams,
A song of many birds,
And every wish and longing seems
Lulled to a numbered flow of words, —
Listen! O, listen!
Here ever hum the golden bees
Underneath full-blossomed trees,
At once with golden fruit and flowers crowned; —
The sand is so smooth, the yellow sand,
That thy keel will not grate, as it touches the land;
All around, with a slumberous sound,
The singing waves slide up the strand,
And there, where the smooth wet pebbles be,
The waters gurgle longingly,

As if they fain would seek the shore,
To be at rest from the ceaseless roar,
To be at rest for evermore, —
For evermore.
Thus, on Life's gloomy sea,
Heareth the marinere
Voices sweet, from far and near,
Ever singing in his ear,
'Here is rest and peace for thee!'

J. R. LOWELL.

THE CHAPEL BY THE SHORE.

BY the shore, a plot of ground
Clips a ruined chapel round,
Buttressed with a grassy mound;
Where day and night and day go by,
And bring no touch of human sound.

Washing of the lonely seas, —
Shaking of the guardian trees, —
Piping of the salted breeze, —
And day and night and day go by,
To the endless tune of these.

Or when winds and waters keep
A hush more dead than any sleep,

Still morns to stiller evenings creep,
  And day and night and day go by;
Here the stillness is most deep.

And the ruins, lapsed again
Into Nature's wide domain,
Sow themselves with seed and grain,
  As day and night and day go by,
And hoard June's sun and April's rain.

Here fresh funeral tears were shed;
And now the graves are also dead;
And suckers from the ash-tree spread,
  As day and night and day go by,
And stars move calmly overhead.

W. ALLINGHAM.

THE BAY OF NAPLES.

THE sun is warm, the sky is clear,
  The waves are dancing fast and bright,
Blue isles and snowy mountains wear
  The purple noon's transparent light:
The breath of the moist air is light,
  Around its unexpanded buds;
Like many a voice of one delight,
  The winds, the birds, the ocean floods,
The City's voice itself is soft, like Solitude's.

I see the Deep's untrampled floor
With green and purple sea-weeds strown;
I see the waves upon the shore,
Like light dissolved in star-showers, thrown;
I sit upon the sands alone,
The lightning of the noon-tide ocean
Is flashing round me, and a tone
Arises from its measured motion,
How sweet! did any heart now share in my emotion.

Alas! I have nor hope nor health,
Nor peace within nor calm around,
Nor that content surpassing wealth
The sage in meditation found,
And walked with inward glory crowned —
Nor fame, nor power, nor love, nor leisure.
Others I see whom these surround —
Smiling they live, and call life pleasure;
To me that cup has been dealt in another measure.

Yet now despair itself is mild,
Even as the winds and waters are;
I could lie down like a tired child,
And weep away the life of care
Which I have borne and yet must bear,
Till death like sleep might steal on me,
And I might feel in the warm air
My cheek grow cold, and hear the sea
Breathe o'er my dying brain its last monotony.

Some might lament that I were cold,
As I when this sweet day is gone,

Which my lost heart, too soon grown old,
  Insults with this untimely moan;
They might lament — for I am one
  Whom men love not, — and yet regret,
Unlike this day, which, when the sun
  Shall on its stainless glory set,
Will linger, though enjoyed, like joy in memory yet.

SHELLEY.

FISHER'S SONG.

UP and down, all day long,
Life glides by us, like our song;
    In our little fisher-boat,
    On the restless sea we float,
Up and down, all day long,
Life glides by us, like our song.

Far from care, far from pain,
Far from thoughts of greedy gain,
    Calmly, cheerfully we ride
    Over life's tempestuous tide,
Far from care, far from pain,
Far from thoughts of greedy gain.

From the German.

SONG.

Rushes lean over the water,
  Shells lie on the shore,
And thou, the blue Ocean's daughter,
  Sleep'st soft in the song of its roar.

Clouds sail over the ocean,
  White gusts fleck its calm,
But never its wildest motion
  Thy beautiful rest should harm.

White feet on the edge of the billow
  Mock its smooth-seething cream ;
Hard ribs of beach-sand thy pillow,
  And a noble lover thy dream.

Like tangles of sea-weed streaming
  Over a perfect pearl,
Thy fair hair fringes thy dreaming,
  O sleeping Lido girl !

G. W. Curtis.

THE CORAL GROVE.

Deep in the wave is a coral grove,
Where the purple mullet and gold-fish rove,
Where the sea-flower spreads its leaves of blue,
That never are wet with falling dew,
But in bright and changeful beauty shine,
Far down in the green and glassy brine.
The floor is of sand, like the mountain drift,
And the pearl-shells spangle the flinty snow;
From coral rocks the sea-plants lift
Their boughs, where the tides and billows flow;
The water is calm and still below,
For the winds and the waves are absent there,
And the sands are bright as the stars that glow
In the motionless fields of upper air:
There, with its waving blade of green,
The sea-flag streams through the silent water,
And the crimson leaf of the dulse is seen
To blush like a banner bathed in slaughter:
There, with a light and easy motion,
The fan-coral sweeps through the clear deep sea;
And the yellow and scarlet tufts of ocean
Are bending like corn on the upland lea:

And life, in rare and beautiful forms,
Is sporting amid those bowers of stone,
And is safe when the wrathful spirit of storms
Has made the top of the waves his own:
And when the ship from his fury flies,
When the myriad voices of Ocean roar,
When the wind-god frowns in the murky skies,
And demons are waiting the wreck on shore;
Then, far below, in the peaceful sea,
The purple mullet and gold-fish rove,
Where the waters murmur tranquilly,
Through the bending twigs of the coral grove.

J. G. Percival.

THE SONG OF THE SEA-SHELL.

I came from the ocean, a billow past o'er me,
  And, covered with sea-weeds and glittering foam,
I fell on the sands, and a stranger soon bore me,
  To deck the gay halls of his far distant home.
Encompassed by exquisite myrtles and roses,
  Still, still in the deep I am pining to be,
And the low voice within me my feeling discloses,
  And evermore murmurs the sound of the sea.

The skylark at morn pours a carol of pleasure,
  At eve the sad nightingale warbles her note;
The harp in our halls nightly sounds a glad measure,
  And beauty's sweet songs on the air lightly float.

Yet I sigh for the loud-breaking billows that tost me,
I long to the cool coral caverns to flee ;
And when guests with officious intrusion accost me,
I answer them still in the tones of the sea.

Since I left the blue deep, I am ever regretting,
And, mingled with men in the regions above,
I have known them, the ties they once cherished forgetting,
Oft trust to new friendships and cling to new love.
Oh ! is it so hard to maintain true devotion ?
Let mortals who doubt seek a lesson from me :
I am bound by mysterious ties to the ocean,
And no language is mine but the sound of the sea.

MRS. ABDY.

ON A BOOK OF SEA-MOSSES.

THESE many-colored, variegated forms,
Sail to our rougher shores, and rise and fall
To the deep music of the Atlantic wave.
Such spoils we capture where the rainbows drop,
Melting in ocean. Here are broideries strange,
Wrought by the sea-nymphs from their golden hair,
And wove by moonlight. Gently turn the leaf.
From narrow cells, scooped in the rocks, we take

These fairy textures, lightly moored at morn.
Down sunny slopes outstretching to the deep,
We roam at noon, and gather shapes like these.
Note now the painted webs from verdurous isles,
Festooned and spangled in sea-caves, and say
What hues of land can rival tints like those,
Torn from the scarfs and gonfalons of kings
Who dwell beneath the waters?

J. T. Fields.

ARIEL'S SONGS.

I.

Come unto these yellow sands,
And then take hands:
Court'sied when you have and kiss'd,
(The wild waves whist!)
Foot it featly here and there;
And sweet sprites, the burden bear.
Hark, hark!
Bowgh, wowgh. [*dispersedly.*
The watch-dogs bark.
Bowgh, wowgh. [*dispersedly.*
Hark, hark! I hear
The strain of strutting chanticleer
Cry, Cock-a-doodle-doo.

II.

Full fathom five thy father lies,
Of his bones are coral made;
Those are pearls that were his eyes;
Nothing of him that doth fade,
But doth suffer a sea-change
Into something rich and strange.
Sea-nymphs hourly ring his knell:
[*Burden, ding-dong.*
Hark, now I hear them;—ding, dong, bell!

SHAKSPEARE.

GULF-WEED.

A WEARY weed, tossed to and fro,
Drearily drenched in the ocean brine,
Soaring high and sinking low,
Lashed along without will of mine;
Sport of the spoom of the surging sea,
Flung on the foam, afar and anear;
Mark my manifold mystery,
Growth and grace in their place appear.

I bear round berries, grey and red,
Rootless and rover though I be;
My spangled leaves, when nicely spread,
Arboresce as a trunkless tree;

Corals curious coat me o'er
White and hard in apt array;
Mid the wild waves' rude uproar,
Gracefully grow I, night and day.

Hearts there are on the sounding shore,
(Something whispers soft to me,)
Restless and roaming for evermore,
Like this weary weed of the sea;
Bear they yet on each beating breast,
The eternal Type of the wondrous whole,
Growth unfolding amidst unrest,
Grace informing with silent soul.

C. G. Fenner.

I SAW FROM THE BEACH.

I saw from the beach, when the morning was shining,
A bark o'er the waters move gloriously on;
I came, when the sun o'er that beach was declining, —
The bark was still there, but the waters were gone!

Ah! such is the fate of our life's early promise;
So passing the spring-tide of joy we have known:
Each wave, that we danced o'er at morning, ebbs from us,
And leaves us at eve, on the bleak shore alone!

Ne'er tell me of glories serenely adorning
  The close of our day, the calm eve of our night,—
Give me back, give me back the wild freshness of morning,
  Her clouds and her tears are worth evening's best light.

Oh, who would not welcome that moment's returning,
  When passion first waked a new life thro' his frame,
And his soul,—like the wood that grows precious in burning,—
  Gave out all its sweets to Love's exquisite flame!

MOORE.

SONG.

SWEET and low, sweet and low,
  Wind of the western sea,
Low, low, breathe and blow,
  Wind of the western sea!
Over the rolling waters go;
Come from the dying moon, and blow,
  Blow him again to me;
While my little one, while my pretty one sleeps.

Sleep and rest, sleep and rest,
  Father will come to thee soon;

Rest, rest, on mother's breast,
  Father will come to thee soon,
Father will come to his babe in the nest:
Silver sails all out of the west
  Under the silver moon:
Sleep, my little one, sleep, my pretty one, sleep.

ALFRED TENNYSON.

THE MARINER.

YE winds that sweep the grove's green tops
  And kiss the mountains hoar,
O softly stir the ocean-waves
  That sweep along the shore!
For my love sails the fairest ship
  That wantons on the sea;
O bend his masts with pleasant gales,
  And waft him hame to me.

O leave nae mair the bonny glen,
  Clear stream, and hawthorn grove,
Where first we walked in gloaming gray,
  And sighed and looked of love;
For faithless is the ocean wave,
  And faithless is the wind:
Then leave nae mair my heart to break
  'Mang Scotland's hills behind.

ALLAN CUNNINGHAM.

BALLAD.

Oh, why does my lover linger,
  The lover that loves me well,
In bowers under the blue waves,
  Lull'd by a breathing shell?

Why waits he among the corals,
  In the cold sea-deeps alone,
While the shore is tired with my foot-tread,
  The wind sick with my moan?

My rose-woven wreath is fallen,
  My hair all damp and torn,
My bridal garments fading,
  Their silver white is gone.

Yet in bowers under the blue waves,
  Lull'd by a breathing shell,
While my bridal garments fade, waits
  The lover that loves me well.

Oh, fairer than our palm-groves
  The ruby corals must be ; —
He will not leave their cool shades
  For even his love of me !

Yet far, far over the ocean
  Left he his mother dear,
And his father's grave, and promised
  To dwell forever here.

And over the wide, wide ocean
  His dark-eyed sister left he,
To mourn for him, and promised
  Forever to dwell with me.

Then dearer than his youth's bowers
  The ruby corals must be,
Since he will not leave their cool shades
  For even his love of me.

James W. Miller.

I would take thee home to my heart, but thou wilt not come to me :
Ah ! lonely art thou sailing far out on the stormy sea ;
And lonely am I sitting with the cold dark rocks around ;
Weary the sight of heaving waves, weary their thundering sound.

Anonymous.

ANNIE OF LOCHROYAN.

'O WHA will shoe my bonny foot?
And wha will glove my hand?
And wha will lace my middle jimp
Wi' a lang lang linen band?

'O wha will kame my yellow hair
Wi' a new-made silver kame?
And wha will be my bairn's father
Till Lord Gregory come hame?'

'Thy father will shoe thy bonny foot,
Thy mother will glove thy hand,
Thy sister will lace thy middle jimp
Wi' a lang lang linen band.

'Thy brother will kame thy yellow hair,
Wi' a new-made silver kame,
And God will be thy bairn's father,
Till Lord Gregory come hame.'

'But I will get a bonny boat,
  And I will sail the sea,
And I will gang to Lord Gregory
  Since he canna come to me.'

Syne she's gar'd build a bonny boat
  To sail the salt salt sea ;
The sails were o' the gude green silk,
  The tows o' taffety.

She hadna sailed but twenty leagues,
  But twenty leagues and three,
When she met wi' a rank robber,
  And a' his company.

'Now whether are ye the queen hersell,
  (For so ye well might be,)
Or are ye the lass o' Lochroyan,
  Seekin' Lord Gregory ?'

'O I am not the queen,' she said,
  Nor sic I seem to be,
'But I am Annie of Lochroyan
  Seekin' Lord Gregory.'

'O see ye na yon stately tower,
  That's covered o'er wi' tin ;
When thou hast sailed it round about,
  Lord Gregory is within.'

And when she saw the stately tower
  Shining so clear and bright,
That stood aboon the jarring wave
  Built on a rock of height;

Says;—'Row the boat, my mariners,
  And bring me to the land,
For yonder I spy my love's castle,
  Close by the salt sea strand.'

She sailed it round, and sailed it round,
  And loud loud cried she,
'Now break, now break, ye fairy charms,
  And set my true love free!'

She's ta'en her young son in her arms,
  And to the door she's gane;
And lang she knocked, and sair she ca'd,
  But answer got she nane.

'O open the door, Lord Gregory!
  O open and let me in!
For the wind blaws through my yellow hair,
  And the rain drops o'er my chin.'

'Awa, awa, ye ill woman,
  Ye're no come here for good,
Ye're but some witch, or wild warlock,
  Or mermaid o' the flood.'

'I am neither witch, nor wild warlock,
Nor mermaid o' the sea,
But I am Annie of Lochroyan;
O open the door to me!'

'Gin thou be the lass o' Lochroyan,
(As I trow thou binna she,)
Tell me some of the love-tokens,
That pass'd between thee and me.'

'O dinna ye mind, Lord Gregory,
As we sat at the wine,
We changed the rings from our fingers,
And I can show thee thine?

'O yours was gude, and gude enough,
But aye the best was mine;
Yours was o' the gude red gowd,
But mine o' the diamond fine.

'Now open the door, Lord Gregory!
Open the door, I pray!
For thy young son is in my arms,
And will be dead ere day.'

'If thou be Annie of Lochroyan,
(As I kenna thou be,)
Tell me some mair o' the love-tokens,
That pass'd between me and thee.'

Fair Annie turned her round about: —
 'And O! if it be sae,
May never a woman that has borne a son
 Hae a heart sae fou o' wae!

'Take down, take down, that mast o' gowd!
 Set up a mast o' tree!
It disna become a forsaken lady
 To sail sae royally!'

When the cock had crawn and the day did dawn,
 And the sun began to peep,
Then up and raise him Lord Gregory
 And sair sair did he weep.

'O I hae dreamed a dream, mother,
 I wish it may prove true!
That the bonny lass o' Lochroyan
 Was at the door e'en now.

'O I hae dreamed a dream, mother,
 The thought o't gars me greet!
That fair Annie o' Lochroyan
 Lay cauld dead at my feet.'

'Gin it be for Annie of Lochroyan,
 That ye make a' this din,
She stood a' last night at your door,
 But I trow she wan na in.'

'O wae betide ye, ill woman!
An ill death may ye die!
That wadna open the door to her,
Nor yet wad waken me!'

O he's gane down to yon shore side
As fast as he can fare;
He saw fair Annie in the boat
But the wind it rocked her sair.

'And hey, Annie, and how, Annie!
O Annie, winna ye bide?'
But aye the mair he cried Annie,
The braider grew the tide.

'And hey, Annie, and how, Annie,
Dear Annie, speak to me!'
But aye the louder he cried Annie,
The louder roared the sea.

The wind blew loud, the sea grew rough
And dashed the boat on the shore;
Fair Annie floated through the faem,
But the babie rose no more.

Lord Gregory tore his yellow hair,
And made a heavy moan,
Fair Annie's corse lay at his feet,
Her fair young son was gone.

O cherry, cherry was her cheek,
  And gowden was her hair,
But clay cold were her rosy lips,
  Nae spark o' life was there.

And first he kissed her cherry cheek,
  And syne he kissed her chin,
And syne he kissed her rosy lips, —
  There was nae breath within.

'O wae betide my cruel mother!
  An ill death may she die!
She turned my true love frae my door,
  Wha came sae far to me.

'O wae betide my cruel mother,
  An ill death maun she die!
She turned fair Annie from my door,
  Wha died for love o' me.'

Scottish Border Minstrelsy.

[Glossary. — *Jimp*, slender ; *tows*, ropes ; *jawing*, dashing.]

COME O'ER THE SEA.

Come o'er the sea,
Maiden! with me,
Mine through sunshine, storm, and snows.
Seasons may roll,
But the true soul
Burns the same where'er it goes.
Let fate frown on, so we love and part not;
'Tis life where thou art, 'tis death where thou art not!
Then come o'er the sea,
Maiden! with me;
Come wherever the wild wind blows.
Seasons may roll,
But the true soul
Burns the same where'er it goes.

Is not the sea
Made for the free,
Land, for courts and chains alone?
Here we are slaves,
But on the waves,
Love and liberty's all our own.

No eye to watch, and no tongue to wound us,
All earth forgot, and all heaven around us!
Then come o'er the sea,
Maiden! with me;
Come wherever the wild wind blows.
Seasons may roll,
But the true soul
Burns the same where'er it goes.

MOORE.

BY THE ROLLING WAVES.

By the rolling waves I roam,
And look along the sea,
And dream of the day and the gleaming sail,
That bore my love from me.

His bark now sails the Indian seas,
Far down the summer zone:
But his thoughts, like swallows, fly to me
By the northern waves alone

Nor will he delay, when winds are fair,
To waft him back to me;
But haste, my love! or my grave will be made,
By the sad and moaning sea.

R. H. STODDARD.

SONG.

Come on the bright sea lonely,
    O maiden fair and free,
Come homeless and friendless, and only
    With me, with me!
My boat on the blue wave heaves:
    See! what a fairy thing,
With its pennons, mast, and keel;
'Tis but a little shell —
    But there *I* am king!

The Earth is made for the slave,
    O maiden free!
But for man, the true and brave,
    The boundless sea;
Waves whisper in their flow
    A mystery
Of a secret spell they know,
Of Life and of Love, and oh!
    Of Liberty!

From the French of De Vigny.

O MAID OF ISLA.

O Maid of Isla, from the cliff
  That looks on troubled wave and sky,
Dost thou not see yon little skiff
  Contend with ocean gallantly?
Now beating 'gainst the breeze and surge,
  And steeped her leeward deck in foam,
Why does she war unequal urge? —
  O Isla's maid, she seeks her home!

O Isla's maid, yon sea-bird mark!
  Her white wing gleams through mist and spray
Against the storm-cloud lowering dark,
  As to the rock she wheels away.
Where clouds are dark and billows rave,
  Why to the shelter should she come
Of cliff, exposed to wind and wave? —
  O maid of Isla, 'tis her home!

Scott.

SONG.

Our boat to the waves go free,
By the bending tide, where the curled wave breaks,
Like the track of the wind on the white snow-flakes;
Away! away! 'Tis a path o'er the sea.

Blasts may rave! — spread the sail,
For our spirits can wrest the power from the wind,
And the gray clouds yield to the sunny mind;
Fear not we the whirl of the gale.

Waves on the beach, and the wild sea-foam,
With a leap, and a dash, and a sudden cheer,
Where the sea-weed makes its bending home,
And the sea-birds swim on the crests so clear,
Wave after wave, they are curling o'er,
Where the white sand dazzles along the shore.

W. E. Channing.

BALLAD.

He stood on the rock,
And he looked on the sea,
And he said of his false Love,
'My Love, where is she?'

'Have they bought her with bracelets
And lured her with gold?
Is her love for her lover
A tale that is told?'

From the crest of the wave,
In the deep of the gulf,
Came a voice that cried, 'Save!
For behold the sea-wolf!'

He stood on the rock,
And he looked on the wave,
And he said, 'Oh! St. Ulfrid,
Who's this that cries, Save!'

Then arose from the billow,
A head with a crown,
And two hands that divided
The hair falling down.

As the foam in the moonlight
The two hands were fair,
And they put by the tangles
Of sea-weed and hair.

He knew the pale forehead—
A spell to his ear
Was the voice that repeated,
'The sea-wolf is here!'

'I come, Love,' he answered;—
At sunrise next day
A fisherman wakened
The Priest in the Bay.

'For the soul of a sinner
Let masses be said—
The sin shall be nameless,
And nameless the dead.'

HENRY TAYLOR.

NIGHT AND MORNING.

I.

THE grey sea and the long black land;
And the yellow half-moon, large and low;
And the startled little waves that leap
In fiery ringlets from their sleep,
As I gain the cove with pushing prow,
And quench its speed in the slushy sand.

Then a mile of warm sea-scented beach;
Three fields to cross till a farm appears;
A tap at the pane, the quick, sharp scratch
And blue spurt of a lighted match,
And a voice less loud, through its joys and fears,
Than the two hearts beating each to each!

II.

Round the cape of a sudden came the sea,
And the sun looked over the mountain's rim,
And straight was a path of gold for him,
And the need of a world of men for me.

ROBERT BROWNING.

LEANDER SWIMMING.

Then at the flame a torch fair Hero lit,
And o'er her head anxiously holding it,
Ascended to the roof; and leaning there,
Lifted its light into the darksome air.

The boy beheld, — beheld it from the sea,
And parted his wet locks, and breathed with glee,
And rose, in swimming, more triumphantly.

Smooth was the sea that night, the lover strong,
And in the springy waves he danced along.
He rose, he dipped his breast, he aimed, he cut
With his clear arms, and from before him put
The parting waves, and in and out the air
His shoulders felt, and trailed his washing hair;
But when he saw the torch, oh! how he sprung,
And thrust his feet against the waves, and flung
The foam behind, as though he scorned the sea,
And parted his wet locks, and breathed with glee,
And rose, and panted, most triumphantly!

Arrived at last on shallow ground, he saw
The stooping light, as if in haste, withdraw;
Again it issued just above the door
With a white hand, and vanished as before.
Then rising, with a sudden-ceasing sound
Of wateriness, he stood on the firm ground,
And treading up a little slippery bank,
With jutting myrtles mixed, and verdure dank,
Came to a door ajar, — all hushed, all blind
With darkness; yet he guessed who stood behind;
And entering with a turn, the breathless boy
A breathless welcome finds, and words that die for joy.

LEIGH HUNT.

IS MY LOVER ON THE SEA?

Is my lover on the sea?
  Sailing east, or sailing west?
Mighty Ocean, gentle be,
  Rock him into rest!

Let no angry wind arise,
  Nor a wave with whitened crest;
All be gentle as his eyes,
  When he is caressed!

BARRY CORNWALL.

THE PLEASURE-BOAT.

Come, hoist the sail, the fast let go!
  They're seated side by side;
Wave chases wave in pleasant flow:
  The bay is fair and wide.

The ripples lightly tap the boat.
  Loose! — Give her to the wind!
She shoots ahead: — they're all afloat:
  The strand is far behind.

No danger reach so fair a crew;
  Thou goddess of the foam,
I'll ever pay thee worship due,
  If thou wilt bring them home.

Fair ladies, fairer than the spray
  The prow is dashing wide,
Soft breezes take you on your way,
  Soft flow the blessed tide!

O, might I like those breezes be,
  And touch that arching brow,
I'd toil for ever on the sea
  Where ye are floating now.

The boat goes tilting on the waves;
  The waves go tilting by;
There dips the duck: — her back she laves;
  O'erhead the sea-gulls fly.

Now, like the gulls that dart for prey,
  The little vessel stoops;
Now rising, shoots along her way,
  Like them, in easy swoops.

The sun-light falling on her sheet,
  It glitters like the drift
Sparkling in scorn of summer's heat,
  High up some mountain rift.

The winds are fresh; she's driving fast
  Upon the bending tide,
The crinkling sail, and crinkling mast,
  Go with her side by side.

Why dies the breeze away so soon?
  Why hangs the pennant down?
The sea is glass; the sun at noon.
  — Nay, lady, do not frown;

For, see, the winged fisher's plume
  Is painted on the sea:
Below, a cheek of lovely bloom.
  — Whose eyes look up at thee?

She smiles; thou need'st must smile on her;
  And, see, beside her face
A rich, white cloud that doth not stir.
  What beauty, and what grace!

And pictured beach of yellow sand,
  And peaked rock, and hill,
Change the smooth sea to fairy land.
  How lovely and how still!

From that far isle the thresher's flail
  Strikes close upon the ear;
The leaping fish, the swinging sail
  Of yonder sloop sound near.

The parting sun sends out a glow
  Across the placid bay,
Touching with glory all the show. —
  A breeze! — Up helm! — Away!

Careening to the wind, they reach,
  With laugh and call, the shore.
They've left their foot-prints on the beach;
  But *them* I hear no more.

Goddess of Beauty, must I now
  Vowed worship to thee pay?
Dear goddess, I grow old, I trow:
  My head is growing grey.

R. H. Dana.

MERRILY BOUNDS THE BARK.

Merrily, merrily bounds the bark,
  She bounds before the gale;
The mountain breeze from Ben-na-darch
  Is joyous in her sail.

With fluttering sound, like laughter hoarse,
  The cords and canvas strain;
The waves, divided by her force,
In rippling eddies chase her course,
  As if they laugh'd again.

Merrily, merrily bounds the bark,
  O'er the broad ocean driven;
Her path by Ronin's mountain dark,
  The steersman's hand has given.

Merrily, merrily goes the bark,
  On a breeze from the northward free,
So shoots through the morning sky the lark,
  Or the swan through the summer sea.

Merrily, merrily, goes the bark,
  Before the gale she bounds;
So flies the dolphin from the shark,
  Or the deer before the hounds.

SCOTT.

THE INCHCAPE ROCK.

No stir in the air, no stir in the sea,
The ship was still as she might be;
Her sails from heaven received no motion —
Her keel was steady in the ocean.

Without either sign or sound of their shock,
The waves flowed over the Inchcape Rock;
So little they rose, so little they fell,
They did not move the Inchcape Bell.

The holy abbot of Aberbrothok
Had floated that bell on the Inchcape Rock;
On the waves of the storm it floated and swung,
And louder and louder its warning rung.

When the rock was hid by the tempest's swell,
The mariners heard the warning bell;
And then they knew the perilous Rock,
And bless'd the priest of Aberbrothok.

The sun in heaven shone so gay —
All things were joyful on that day:
The sea-birds scream'd as they sported round,
And there was pleasure in their sound.

The float of the Inchcape Bell was seen,
A darker speck on the ocean green;
Sir Ralph the Rover walk'd his deck,
And he fix'd his eye on the darker speck.

He felt the cheering power of Spring,
It made him whistle, it made him sing;
His heart was mirthful to excess —
But the Rover's mirth was wickedness.

His eye was on the bell and float —
Quoth he, my men, pull out the boat,
And row me to the Inchcape Rock,
And I'll plague the priest of Aberbrothok.

The boat is lowered, the boatmen row,
And to the Inchcape Rock they go;
Sir Ralph bent over from the boat,
And cut the warning bell from the float.

Down sunk the bell with a gurgling sound;
The bubbles rose, and burst aground.
Quoth Sir Ralph, the next who comes to the Rock
Will not bless the priest of Aberbrothok.

Sir Ralph the Rover sail'd away;
He scour'd the seas for many a day;
And now, grown rich with plunder'd store,
He steers his course to Scotland's shore.

So thick a haze o'erspreads the sky,
They could not see the sun on high;
The wind hath blown a gale all day;
At evening it hath died away.

On the deck the Rover takes his stand;
So dark it is, they see no land;
Quoth Sir Ralph, it will be lighter soon,
For there is the dawn of the rising moon.

Canst hear, said one, the breakers roar?
For yonder, methinks, should be the shore.
Now where we are I cannot tell,
But I wish we could hear the Inchcape Bell.

They hear no sound, the swell is strong,
Though the wind hath fallen they drift along,
Till the vessel strikes with a shivering shock—
Oh, Christ! it is the Inchcape Rock!

SOUTHEY.

THE STEAM-BOAT.

See how yon flaming herald treads
  The ridged and rolling waves,
As, crashing o'er their crested heads,
  She bows her surly slaves.
With foam before and fire behind,
  She rends the clinging sea
That flies before the roaring wind,
  Beneath her hissing lee.

The morning spray, like sea-born flowers,
  With heaped and glistening bells,
Falls round her fast, in ringing showers,
  With every wave that swells;
And flaming o'er the midnight deep,
  In lurid fringes thrown,
The living gems of ocean sweep
  Along her flashing zone.

With clashing wheel and lifting keel,
  And smoking torch on high,
When winds are loud and billows reel,
  She thunders foaming by;

When seas are silent and serene,
  With even beam she glides,
The sunshine glimmering through the green,
  That skirts her gleaming sides.

Now like a wild nymph, far apart,
  She veils her shadowy form,
The beating of her restless heart
  Still sounding through the storm ; —
Now answers, like a courtly dame,
  The reddening surges o'er,
With flying scarf of spangled flame
  The Pharos of the shore.

To-night yon pilot shall not sleep
  Who trims his narrowed sail,
To-night yon frigate scarce can keep
  Her broad breast to the gale ;
And many a foresail, scooped and strained,
  Shall break from yard and stay,
Before this smoky wreath has stained
  The rising mist of day.

Hark, hark, I hear yon whistling shroud,
  I see yon quivering mast ;
The black throat of the hunted cloud
  Is panting forth the blast !
An hour, and whirled like winnowing chaff,
  The giant surge shall fling
His tresses o'er yon pennon-staff,
  White as the sea-bird's wing !

Yet rest, ye wanderers of the deep;
Nor wind nor wave shall tire
Those fleshless arms, whose pulses leap
With floods of living fire.
Sleep on; and when the morning light
Streams o'er the shining bay,
O think of those for whom the night
Shall never wake in day!

O. W. Holmes.

A MORNING SCENE.

Amid the rosy fog stole in and out
The little boat; the rower dipped his oar,
Gleaming with liquid gold; and all about
The red-sailed ships went swimming from the shore.

Against the canvas, moving to and fro,
The dark forms of the fishermen were seen;
Around the prow long wreaths of golden glow
Rippled and faded 'mid the wavy green.

The sea-gulls wheeled around the rocky cape,
And skimmed their long wings lightly o'er the flood;
The fog rose up in many a spectral shape,
And crept away in silence o'er the wood.

The sea, from silvery white to deepest blue,
Changed 'neath the changing colors of the sky;
The distant light-house broke upon the view,
And the long land-point spread before the eye.

Clear as a mirror lay the rock-bound cove;
Far off, one blasted pine against the sky
Lifted its scraggy form; the crow above
Flapped his black wings, and wound his long shrill cry.

I paced the beach like some sleep-waking child,
Wrapped in a dream of beauty and of awe;
Were they ideal visions that beguiled?
Was it my eye, or but my soul that saw?

SARAH C. E. MAYO.

SUNRISE ON THE SEA-COAST.

It was the holy hour of dawn:
By hands invisible withdrawn,
The curtain of the summer night
Had vanished; and the morning light,
Fresh from its hidden day-springs, threw
Increasing glory up the blue.
O sacred balm of summer dawn,
When odors from the new-mown lawn

Blend with the breath of sky and sea,
And like the prayers of sanctity,
Go up to Him who reigns above,
An incense-offering of love!

Alone upon a rock I stood,
Far out above the ocean-flood,
Whose vast expanse before me lay,
Now silver-white, now leaden-gray,
As o'er its face alternate threw
The rays and clouds their varying hue.

I felt a deep, expectant hush
Through nature, as the increasing flush
Of the red Orient seemed to tell
The approach of some great spectacle,
O'er which the birds in heaven's far height
Hung, as entranced, in mute delight.
But when the sun, in royal state
Through his triumphant golden gate,
Came riding forth in majesty
Out of the fleckéd Eastern sky,
As comes a conqueror to his tent;
And up and down the firmament,
The captive clouds of routed night,
Their garments fringed with golden light
Bending around the azure arch,
Lent glory to the victor's march;
And when he flung his blazing glance
Across the watery expanse,—
Methought, along that rocky coast,
The foaming waves, a crested host,

As on their snowy plumes the beams
Of sunshine fell in dazzling gleams,
Thrilled through their ranks with wild delight,
And clapped their hands to hail the sight,
And sent a mighty shout on high
Of exultation to the sky!

. . . . . .

O Father! 'tis on Thee I call;
Father of lights! revealed in all.
To live in nature and in Thee!
I am Thy child: Oh! let me hear
Thy voice and feel Thy footstep near.
And as, upon my bended brow,
It comes with holy influence now,
So, Father! may Thy gentle breath
Refresh me in the hour of death!
Then be my feverish temples fanned
With breezes from that unseen land,—
With morning breezes from the shore
Where death and darkness dwell no more,
And dawnings of eternal light
Prevent the steps of life's last night!

C. T. Brooks.

THE LIGHT-HOUSE.

The rocky ledge runs far into the sea,
  And on its outer point, some miles away,
The Light-house lifts its massive masonry,
  A pillar of fire by night, of cloud by day.

Even at this distance I can see the tides,
  Upheaving, break unheard along its base,
A speechless wrath, that rises and subsides
  In the white lip and tremor of the face.

And as the evening darkens, lo! how bright,
  Through the deep purple of the twilight air,
Beams forth the sudden radiance of its light
  With strange, unearthly splendor in its glare!

Not one alone; from each projecting cape
  And perilous reef along the ocean's verge,
Starts into life a dim, gigantic shape,
  Holding its lantern o'er the restless surge.

Like the great giant Christopher it stands
  Upon the brink of the tempestuous wave,
Wading far out among the rocks and sands,
  The night-o'ertaken mariner to save.

And the great ships sail outward and return,
  Bending and bowing o'er the billowy swells,
And ever joyful, as they see it burn,
  They wave their silent welcomes and farewells.

They come forth from the darkness, and their sails
  Gleam for a moment only in the blaze,
And eager faces, as the light unveils,
  Gaze at the tower, and vanish while they gaze.

The mariner remembers when a child,
  On his first voyage, he saw it fade and sink;
And when, returning from adventures wild,
  He saw it rise again o'er ocean's brink.

Steadfast, serene, immovable, the same
  Year after year, through all the silent night
Burns on for evermore that quenchless flame,
  Shines on that inextinguishable light!

It sees the ocean to its bosom clasp
  The rocks and sea-sand with the kiss of peace;
It sees the wild winds lift it in their grasp,
  And hold it up, and shake it like a fleece.

The startled waves leap over it; the storm
  Smites it with all the scourges of the rain,
And steadily against its solid form
  Press the great shoulders of the hurricane.

The sea-bird wheeling round it, with the din
  Of wings, and winds, and solitary cries,
Blinded and maddened by the light within,
  Dashes himself against the glare, and dies.

A new Prometheus, chained upon the rock,
  Still grasping in his hand the fire of Jove,
It does not hear the cry, nor heed the shock,
  But hails the mariner with words of love.

'Sail on!' it says, 'sail on, ye stately ships!
  And with your floating bridge the ocean span;
Be mine to guard this light from all eclipse,
  Be yours to bring man nearer unto man!'

H. W. LONGFELLOW.

THE SEA-MEW.

How joyously the young sea-mew
Lay dreaming on the waters blue,
Whereon our little bark had thrown
A forward shade — the only one —
(But shadows aye will man pursue!)

Familiar with the waves, and free,
As if their own white foam were he:
His heart upon the heart of ocean,
Learning all its mystic motion,
And throbbing to the throbbing sea!

And such a brightness in his eye,
As if the ocean and the sky
Within him had lit up and nurst
A soul God gave him not at first,
To comprehend their majesty.

We were not cruel, yet did sunder
His white wing from the blue waves under,
And bound it — while his fearless eyes
Shone up to ours in calm surprise,
As deeming us some ocean wonder!

We bore our ocean-bird unto
A grassy place, where he might view
The flowers bending to the bees,
The waving of the tall green trees,
The falling of the silver dew.

But flowers of earth were pale to him
Who had seen the rainbow fishes swim;
And when earth's dew around him lay,
He thought of ocean's winged spray,
And his eye waxed sad and dim.

The green trees round him only made
A prison, with their darksome shade;
And droop'd his wing, and mourned he
For his own boundless, glittering sea,—
Albeit he knew not they could fade!

Then one her gladsome face did bring,
Her gentle voice's murmuring,
In ocean's stead his heart to move,
And teach him what was human love,—
He thought it a strange, mournful thing!

He lay down in his grief to die,
(First looking to the sea-like sky
That hath no waves!) because, alas!
Our human touch did on him pass,
And with our touch, our agony.

Elizabeth Barrett Browning.

SONNETS.

I.

WHERE lies the land to which yon ship must go?
Fresh as a lark mounting at break of day,
Festively she puts forth in trim array;
Is she for tropic suns, or polar snow?
What boots the inquiry? — Neither friend nor foe
She cares for; let her travel where she may,
She finds familiar names, a beaten way
Ever before her, and a wind to blow.
Yet, still I ask, what haven is her mark?
And, almost as it was when ships were rare,
(From time to time, like Pilgrims, here and there
Crossing the waters) doubt, and something dark,
Of the old sea some reverential fear,
Is with me at thy farewell, joyous Bark!

II.

With ships the sea was sprinkled far and nigh,
Like stars in heaven, and joyously it showed;
Some lying fast at anchor in the road,
Some veering up and down, one knew not why.
A goodly vessel did I then espy

Come like a giant from a haven broad;
And lustily along the bay she strode,
Her tackling rich, and of apparel high.
This ship was nought to me, nor I to her,
Yet I pursued her with a lover's look;
This ship to all the rest did I prefer:
When will she turn, and whither? She will brook
No tarrying; where she comes the wind must stir:
On went she, and due north her journey took.

III.

Why stand we gazing on the sparkling brine
With wonder smit by its transparency,
And all enraptured with its purity?
Because the unstain'd, the clear, the crystalline,
Have ever in them something of benign,
Whether in gem, in water, or in sky,
A sleeping infant's brow, or wakeful eye
Of a young maiden, only not divine.
Scarcely the hand forbears to dip its palm
For beverage drawn as from a mountain well;
Temptation centres in the liquid calm;
Our daily raiment seems no obstacle
To instantaneous plunging in, deep sea!
And revelling in long embrace with thee.

WORDSWORTH.

THE SEA-KING'S BURIAL.

'My strength is failing fast,'
Said the Sea-king to his men;—
'I shall never sail the seas
Like a conqueror again.
But while yet a drop remains
Of the life-blood in my veins,
Raise, O raise me from the bed;—
Put the crown upon my head;
Put my good sword in my hand;
And so lead me to the strand
Where my ship at anchor rides
Steadily;
If I cannot end my life
In the bloody battle strife,
Let me die as I have lived,
On the sea.'

They have raised King Balder up,
Put his crown upon his head,
They have sheath'd his limbs in mail
And the purple o'er him spread;
And amid the greeting rude
Of a gathering multitude

Borne him slowly to the shore —
All the energy of yore
From his dim eye flashing forth —
Old sea-lion of the north; —
As he looked upon his ship
Riding free,
And on his forehead pale
Felt the cold refreshing gale,
And heard the welcome sound
Of the sea.

. . . . . .

They have borne him to the ship
With a slow and solemn tread;
They have placed him on the deck
With his crown upon his head,
Where he sat as on a throne;
And have left him there alone,
With his anchor ready weigh'd,
And the snowy sail display'd
To the favoring wind once more
Blowing freshly from the shore;
And have bidden him farewell
Tenderly,
Saying, 'King of mighty men,
We shall meet thee yet again,
In Valhalla, with the monarchs
Of the sea.'

Underneath him in the hold
They had placed the lighted brand;
And the fire was burning slow
As the vessel from the land,

Like a stag-hound from the slips,
Darted forth from out the ships; —
There was music in her sail
As it swell'd before the gale,
And a dashing at her prow
As it cleft the waves below,
And the good ship sped along,
Scudding free,
As on many a battle morn
In her time she had been borne,
To struggle and to conquer
On the sea.

And the King with sudden strength
Started up and paced the deck,
With his good sword for his staff,
And his robes around his neck: —
Once alone, he waved his hand
To the people on the land; —
And with shout and joyous cry
Once again they made reply,
Till the loud exulting cheer
Sounded faintly on his ear;
For the gale was o'er him blowing
Fresh and free;
And ere yet an hour had past
He was driven before the blast,
And a storm was on his path,
On the sea.

And still upon the deck —
While the storm about him rent,

King Balder paced about
Till his failing strength was spent.
Then he stopp'd a while to rest —
Cross'd his hands upon his breast,
And look'd upwards to the sky,
With a dim but dauntless eye;
And heard the tall mast creak,
And the fitful tempest speak
Shrill and fierce, to the billows
Rushing free,
And within himself he said,
'I am coming, oh, ye dead!
To join you in Valhalla,
O'er the sea.'

. . . . .

And Balder spake no more,
For his strength began to fail, —
But he look'd upon the sky
As he heard the tempest wail.
To the storm the tall mast bent,
And the sails to shreds were rent;
When from hold and cabin, quick
Rush'd the smoke out, curling thick,
Creeping up amid the shrouds,
Black as wreaths of autumn clouds,
When the lightning from their bosoms
Flashes free;
And the dancing waves upsprung,
And a lurid radiance flung
On the sky, and on the waters
Of the sea.

And Balder moved no limb,
 And no sound escaped his lip;—
And he look'd, yet scarcely saw
 The destruction of his ship:
Nor the fleet sparks mounting high,
Nor the glare upon the sky;—
Scarcely heard the billows dash,
Nor the burning timber crash;—
Scarcely felt the scorching heat
That was gathering at his feet,
Nor the fierce flames mounting o'er him
 Greedily.
But the life was in him yet,
And the courage to forget
All his pain, in his triumph
 On the sea.

Once alone a cry arose,
 Half of anguish, half of pride,
As he sprang upon his feet
 With the flames on every side.
'I am coming!' said the king,
'Where the swords and bucklers ring—
Where the warrior lives again
With the souls of mighty men—
Where the weary find repose,
And the red wine ever flows;—
I am coming, great All-father,
 Unto Thee!
Unto Odin, unto Thor,
And the strong true hearts of yore—
I am coming to Valhalla,
 O'er the sea.'

Red and fierce upon the sky
  Until midnight shone the glare,
And the burning ship drove on
  Like a meteor of the air.
She was driven and hurried past,
Mid the roaring of the blast.
And of Balder, warrior born,
Naught remain'd at break of morn,
On the charr'd and blacken'd hull,
But some ashes and a skull;
And still the vessel drifted
                Heavily.
With a pale and hazy light
Until far into the night,
When the storm had spent its rage,
                On the sea.

Then the ocean ceased her strife
  With the wild winds, lull'd to rest,
And a full, round, placid moon
  Shed a halo on her breast;—
And the burning ship still lay
On the deep sea, far away;—
From her ribs of solid oak,
Pouring forth the flame and smoke;—
Until burnt through all her bulk,
To the water's edge, the hulk
Down a thousand fathoms sank
                Suddenly,

With a low and sullen sound;—
While the billows sang around
Sad requiems for the Monarch
Of the Sea.

CHARLES MACKAY.

SAND-SONG.

SING of Sand!—not such as gloweth
Hot upon the path of the tiger and snake;—
Rather such sand as, when the loud winds wake,
Each ocean-wave knoweth.

Like a Wrath with pinions burning
Travels the red sand of the desert abroad;
While the soft sea-sand glisteneth smooth and untrod,
As eve is returning.

Here is no caravan or camel;
Here the weary mariner alone finds a grave,
Nightly mourned by the moon, that now on yon wave
Sheds a silver enamel.

From the German of F. FREILIGRATH.

SEA-WEED.

When descends on the Atlantic
    The gigantic
Storm-wind of the equinox,
Landward in his wrath he scourges
    The toiling surges,
Laden with sea-weed from the rocks:

From Bermuda's reefs; from edges
    Of sunken ledges,
In some far off, bright Azore;
From Bahama, and the dashing
    Silver-flashing
Surges of San Salvador;

From the tumbling surf, that buries,
    The Orkneyan skerries,
Answering the hoarse Hebrides;
And from wrecks of ships, and drifting
    Spars, uplifting
On the desolate, rainy seas:—

Ever drifting, drifting, drifting,
    On the shifting
Currents of the restless main;
Till in sheltered coves, and reaches
    Of sandy beaches,
All have found repose again.

So when storms of wild emotion
    Strike the ocean
Of the poet's soul, ere long,
From each cave and rocky fastness,
    In its vastness
Floats some fragment of a song;

From the far-off isles enchanted
    Heaven has planted
With the golden fruit of Truth;
From the flashing surf, whose vision
    Gleams Elysian
In the tropic clime of Youth;

From the strong Will, and the Endeavor
    That forever
Wrestles with the tides of Fate;
From the wreck of Hopes far-scattered,
    Tempest-shattered,
Floating waste and desolate:—

Ever drifting, drifting, drifting,
    On the shifting

Currents of the restless heart;
Till at length in books recorded,
    They, like hoarded
Household worlds, no more depart.

H. W. Longfellow.

SONNET.

The world is too much with us; late and soon,
Getting and spending, we lay waste our powers:
Little we see in Nature that is ours;
We have given our hearts away, a sordid boon!
This Sea that bares her bosom to the moon;
The winds that will be howling at all hours,
And are up-gathered now like sleeping flowers;
For this, for every thing, we are out of tune;
It moves us not. — Great God! I'd rather be
A Pagan suckled in a creed outworn;
So might I, standing on this pleasant lea,
Have glimpses that would make me less forlorn;
Have sight of Proteus rising from the sea,
Or hear old Triton blow his wreathéd horn.

Wordsworth.

HOMER.

THE poet, child of heavenly birth,
Is suckled by the mother Earth;
But thy blue bosom, holy Sea!
Cradles his infant fantasy.

The old, blind minstrel on the shore
Stood listening the eternal roar,
And golden ages, long gone by,
Swept bright before his spirit's eye.

On wing of swan the holy flame
Of melodies celestial came,
And Iliad and Odyssey
Rose to the music of the Sea.

From the German of STOLBERG.

THE DESCENT OF NEPTUNE.

THERE sat he high retired from the seas;
There looked with pity on his Grecians beaten;
There burned with rage at the god-king who slew them.
Then rushed he forward from the rugged mountain;
He beat the forest also as he came downward,
And the high cliffs shook underneath his footsteps;
Three times he trod, his fourth step reached his sea-
 home.

There was his palace in the deep sea-water,
Shining with gold and builded firm forever;
And there he yoked him his swift-footed horses
(Their hoofs are brazen, and their manes are golden)
With golden thongs: his golden goad he seizes;
He mounts upon his chariot and doth fly;
Yea, drives he forth his steeds into the billows.

The sea-beasts from the depths rise under him —
They know their King: and the glad sea is parted,
That so his wheels may fly along unhinder'd.
Dry speeds between the waves his brazen axle: —
So bounding fast they bring him to his Grecians.

From HOMER: Iliad vi.

THE BIRTH OF VENUS.

THE ocean stood like crystal. The soft air
Stirred not the glassy waves, but sweetly there
Had rocked itself to slumber. The blue sky
Leaned silently above, and all its high
And azure-circled roof, beneath the wave
Was imaged back, and seemed the deep to pave
With its transparent beauty. While between
The waves and sky, a few white clouds were seen
Floating upon their wings of feathery gold,
As if they knew some charm the universe enrolled.

A holy stillness came, while in the ray
Of heaven's soft light, a delicate foam-wreath lay
Like silver on the sea. Look! look! why shine
Those floating bubbles with such light divine?
They break, and from their mist a lily form
Rises from out the wave, in beauty warm.
The wave is by the blue-veined feet scarce prest,
Her silky ringlets float about her breast,
Veiling its fairy loveliness; while her eye
Is soft and deep as the blue heaven is high.
The Beautiful is born, and sea and earth
May well revere the hour of that mysterious birth.

ANONYMOUS.

SONG.

LOVE still hath something of the sea
  From whence his mother rose;
No time his slaves from doubt can free,
  Nor give their thoughts repose.

They are becalmed in clearest days,
  And in rough weather tost,
They wither under cold delays,
  Or are in tempests lost.

One while they seem to touch the port,
  Then straight into the main
Some angry wind in cruel sport
  The vessel drives again.

At first, disdain and pride they fear,
  Which if they chance to escape,
Rivals and falsehoods soon appear
  In a more dreadful shape.

By such degrees to joy they come,
   And are so long withstood,
So slowly they receive the sum,
   It hardly does them good.

'T is cruel to prolong a pain;
   And to defer a joy,
Believe me, gentle Celemène,
   Offends the winged boy.

An hundred thousand oaths your fears
   Perhaps would not remove;
And, if I gazed a thousand years,
   I could no deeper love.

Sir Charles Sedley.

137

SIREN'S SONG

STEER hither, steer, your winged pines,
  All beaten mariners,
Here lie Love's undiscover'd mines,
  A prey to passengers;
Perfumes far sweeter than the best
Which make the phœnix' urn and nest,
    Fear not your ships,
Nor any to oppose you, save our lips;
    But come on shore
Where no joy dies till love hath gotten more.

For swelling waves, our panting breasts,
  Where never storms arise,
Exchange; and be awhile our guests:
  For stars, gaze on our eyes.
The compass, love shall hourly sing,
And as he goes about the ring,
    We will not miss
To tell each point he nameth with a kiss.

BROWNE.

THE NEREIDS.

BELOVED the last; Beloved the most!
  With willing arms and brow benign
Receive a bosom tempest-tost,
  And bid it ever beat to thine.

The Nereid maids, in days of yore,
  Saw the lost pilot loose the helm,
Saw the wreck blacken all the shore,
  And every wave some head o'erwhelm.

Afar, the youngest of the train
  Beheld (but feared and aided not)
A minstrel from the billowy main
  Borne breathless near her coral grot.

Then terror fled, and pity rose —
  'Ah me!' she cried, 'I come too late!
Rather than not have soothed his woes,
  I would, but may not, share his fate.'

She raised his hand: 'What hand like this
Could reach the heart athwart the lyre!
What lips like these return my kiss,
Or breathe incessant, soft desire!'

From eve to morn, from morn to eve,
She gazed his features o'er and o'er:
And those who love and who believe,
May hear her sigh along the shore.

W. S. Landor.

EVENING ON THE SHORE.

The baffled tides retiring from the land,
Lay bare the beach, and steal the sea-weed's life,
And all is silence, save the gentle strife
Of the spent waters with the yielding sand.

On the tall cliff the dying sunlight glows,
And stains with dolphin hues the waveless bay,—
The stars peep forth that lead the night's array
Where in mid-heaven the deep'ning purple grows.

How cool an eve attends this burning day!
How sweet a peace the troubled wave subdues!
Oh troubled, burning heart! canst thou refuse
To be as calmly hush'd to rest as they?

W. H. Hurlbut.

EVENING VOLUNTARY.

THE sun is couched, the sea-fowl gone to rest,
And the wild storm hath somewhere found a nest;
Air slumbers — wave with wave no longer strives,
Only a heaving of the deep survives,
A tell-tale motion! soon will it be laid,
And by the tide alone the water swayed.
Stealthy withdrawings, interminglings mild,
Of light with shade in beauty reconciled, —
Such is the prospect far as sight can range,
The soothing recompense, the welcome change.
Where now the ships that drove before the blast,
Threatened by angry breakers as they passed,
And by a train of flying clouds bemocked,
Or in the hollow surge at anchor rocked
As on a bed of death? Some lodge in peace,
Saved by His care who bade the tempest cease,
And some, too heedless of past danger, court
Fresh gales to waft them to the far-off port;
But near, or hanging sky and sea between,
Not one of all these winged powers is seen,
Seen in her course, nor mid this quiet heard;
Yet, oh! how gladly would the air be stirred

By some acknowledgment of thanks and praise,
Soft in its temper as those vesper lays
Sung to the Virgin, while accordant oars
Urge the slow bark along Calabrian shores;
A sea-born service, through the mountains felt,
Till into one loved vision all things melt:
Or like those hymns that soothe with graver sound
The gulfy coast of Norway iron-bound;
And from the wide and open Baltic rise
With punctual care, Lutherian harmonies.
Hush, not a voice is here! but why repine
Now when the star of eve comes forth to shine,
On British waters with that look benign?
Ye mariners, that plough your onward way
Or in the haven rest, or sheltering bay,
May silent thanks at least to God be given,
With a full heart; 'our thoughts are heard in Heaven!'

WORDSWORTH.

THE SEA—IN CALM.

Look what immortal floods the sunset pours
Upon us—Mark! how still (as though in dreams
Bound) the once wild and terrible ocean seems!
How silent are the winds! no billow roars;
But all is tranquil as Elysian shores.
The silver margin which aye runneth round
The moon-enchanted sea, hath here no sound:
Even echo speaks not on these radiant moors!

What! is the Giant of the ocean dead,
Whose strength was all unmatched beneath the sun?
No: he reposes! Now his toils are done,
More quiet than the babbling brooks is he.
So mightiest powers by deepest calms are fed,
And sleep, how oft, in things that gentlest be!

Barry Cornwall.

CAPE-COTTAGE AT SUNSET.

We stood upon the ragged rocks,
  When the long day was nearly done;
The waves had ceased their sullen shocks,
  And lapped our feet with murmuring tone,
And o'er the bay in streaming locks
  Blew the red tresses of the sun.

Along the West the golden bars
  Still to a deeper glory grew;
Above our heads the faint, few stars
  Looked out from the unfathomed blue:
And the far city's clamorous jars
  Seemed melted in that evening hue.

O sunset sky! O purple tide!
  O friends to friends that closer pressed!
Those glories have in darkness died,
  And ye have left my longing breast.
I could not keep you by my side,
  Nor fix that radiance in the West.

Upon those rocks the waves shall beat
 With the same low and murmuring strain,
Across those waves, with glancing feet,
 The sunset rays shall seek the main;
But when together shall we meet
 Upon that far-off shore again?

W. B. Glazier.

A SEA-SIDE WALK.

  We walked beside the sea,
After a day which perished silently
Of its own glory, — like the Princess weird,
Who combating the Genius, scorched and seared,
Uttered with burning breath, 'Ho, victory!'
And sank adown, an heap of ashes pale.
  So runs the Arab tale.

  The sky above us showed
An universal and unmoving cloud,
On which the cliffs permitted us to see
Only the outlines of their majesty,
As master-minds, when gazed at by the crowd:
And shining with a gloom, the water gray
  Swang in its morn-taught way.

Nor moon nor stars were out,
They did not dare to tread so soon about,
Though trembling in the footsteps of the sun.
The light was neither night's nor day's, but one
Which, lifelike, had a beauty in its doubt;
And Silence's impassioned breathings round
Seemed wandering into sound.

O solemn-beating heart
Of Nature! I have knowledge that thou art
Bound unto man's by cords he cannot sever,—
And what time they are slackened by him ever,
So to attest his own supernal part,
Still runneth thy vibration, fast and strong,
The slackened cord along.

For though we never spoke
Of the gray water and the shaded rock,—
Dark wave and stone, unconsciously, were fused
Into the plaintive speaking that we used
Of absent friends and memories unforsook;
And, had we seen each other's face, we had
Seen, haply, each was sad.

Elizabeth Barrett Browning.

THE EVENING WIND.

Spirit that breathest through my lattice, thou
  That cool'st the twilight of the sultry day!
Gratefully flows thy freshness round my brow;
  Thou hast been out upon the deep at play,
Riding all day the wild blue waves till now,
  Roughening their crests, and scattering high their
      spray,
And swelling the white sail. I welcome thee
To the scorch'd land, thou wanderer of the sea!

Nor I alone — a thousand bosoms round
  Inhale thee in the fulness of delight;
And languid forms rise up, and pulses bound
  Livelier, at coming of the wind of night;
And languishing to hear thy welcome sound,
  Lies the vast inland, stretch'd beyond the sight.
Go forth, into the gathering shade; go forth, —
God's blessing breathed upon the fainting earth!

Go, rock the little wood-bird in his nest,
  Curl the still waters, bright with stars, and rouse
The wide, old wood from his majestic rest,
  Summoning, from the innumerable boughs,

The strange deep harmonies that haunt his breast:
  Pleasant shall be thy way where meekly bows
The shutting flower, and darkling waters pass,
And where the o'ershadowing branches sweep the grass.

Stoop o'er the place of graves, and softly sway
  The sighing herbage by the gleaming stone;
That they who near the churchyard willows stray,
  And listen in the deepening gloom, alone,
May think of gentle souls that pass'd away,
  Like thy pure breath, into the vast unknown,
Sent forth from heaven among the sons of men,
And gone into the boundless heaven again.

The faint old man shall lean his silver head
  To feel thee; thou shalt kiss the child asleep,
And dry the moisten'd curls that overspread
  His temples, while his breathing grows more deep;
And they who stand about the sick man's bed,
  Shall joy to listen to thy distant sweep,
And softly part his curtains to allow
Thy visit, grateful to his burning brow.

Go — but the circle of eternal change,
  Which is the life of nature, shall restore,
With sounds and scents from all thy mighty range,
  Thee to thy birth-place of the deep once more.
Sweet odors in the sea-air, sweet and strange,
  Shall tell the home-sick mariner of the shore;
And, listening to thy murmur, he shall deem
He hears the rustling leaf and running stream.

W. C. Bryant.

EVENING WALK BY THE BAY.

The evening hour had brought its peace,
Brought end of toil to weary day;
From wearying thoughts to find release,
I sought the sands that skirt the bay.
Dark rain-clouds southward hovering nigh,
Gave to the sea their leaden hue,
But in the west the open sky
Its rose-light on the waters threw.

I stood, with heart more quiet grown,
And watched the pulses of the tide,
The huge black rocks, the sea-weeds brown,
The gray beach stretched on either side,
The boat that dropped its one white sail
Where the steep yellow bank ran down,
And o'er the clump of willows pale
The white towers of the neighboring town.

A cool light brooded o'er the land;
  A changing lustre lit the bay;
The tide just plashed along the sand,
  And voices sounded, far away.
The Past came up to Memory's eye,
  Dark with some clouds of leaden hue,
But many a space of open sky
  Its rose-light on those waters threw.

Then came to me the dearest friend,
  Whose beauteous soul doth, like the sea,
To all things fair new beauty lend,
  Transfiguring the earth to me.
The thoughts that lips could never tell,
  Through subtler senses were made known;
I raised my eyes, — the darkness fell, —
  I stood upon the sands, alone.

SAMUEL LONGFELLOW.

SONNET.

A FAIRER face of evening cannot be:
The holy time is quiet as a nun
Breathless with adoration; the broad sun
Is sinking down in its tranquillity;
The gentleness of heaven broods o'er the sea:
But list! the mighty Being is awake,
And doth with his eternal motion make
A sound like thunder — everlastingly.
Dear Child! dear Girl, that standest with me here!
If thou appear untouch'd with serious thought,
Thy nature is not therefore less divine:
Thou liest in Abraham's bosom all the year;
And worship'st at the Temple's inner shrine,
God being with thee when we know it not.

WORDSWORTH.

VINETA.

Out from the deep, deep caverns of the sea,
 The evening bells are ringing faint and low;
List to the tidings that they bring to thee
 From the old Wonder-City far below.

While 'neath the bosom of the quiet stream
 The circling floods those ancient ruins lave,
Their towers send out a passing golden gleam
 Through the smooth surface of the upper wave.

To glittering waters with enchantments bright,
 Once seen beneath the glow of evening skies,
The sailor oft returns with eager sight,
 Though near his bark the threatening cliffs arise.

Thus from the heart's deep well is music ringing,
 The evening bells are chiming faint and low;
Sweet memories, alas! the charm is bringing
 Of the true love it lived with, long ago!

How fair a world lies here beneath the stream!
Of many hopes its ruins are the grave;
But in the mirror of my happy dream,
Light, as of starry skies, adorns the wave.

Fain am I, then, to dive beneath the glow,
Sink where the waters ever sparkling roll;
For angel voices, chanting sweetly low,
Call me within that City of the Soul.

From the German of UHLAND.

'MUSIC I' THE AIR.'

O LISTEN to the howling sea,
That beats on the remorseless shore;
O listen, for that sound shall be
When our wild hearts shall beat no more.

O listen well and listen long!
For sitting folded close to me,
You could not hear a sweeter song
Than that hoarse murmur of the sea.

GEORGE W. CURTIS.

ELEGIAC.

The winter eve, how soft, how mild!
How calm the earth! how calm the sea!
The earth is like a weary child,
And ocean sings its lullaby.

A little ripple in my ear!
A little motion at my feet!
They only make the quiet here,
Which they disturb not, more complete.

I wander on the sands apart,
I watch the sun, world-wearied, sink
Into his grave; — with tranquil heart
Upon the loved and lost I think.

R. C. Trench.

HYMN.

O UNSEEN Spirit! now a calm divine
 Comes forth from Thee, rejoicing earth and air!
Trees, hills, and houses, all distinctly shine,
 And thy great ocean slumbers every where.

The chime of bells remote, the murmuring sea,
 The song of birds in whispering copse and wood,
The distant voice of children's thoughtless glee,
 And maiden's song, are all one voice of good.

Amid the leaves' green mass a sunny play
 Of flash and shadow, stirs like inward life;
The ship's white sail glides onward far away,
 Unhaunted by a dream of storm or strife.

O Thou! the primal fount of life and peace,
 Who shed'st thy breathing quiet all around,
In me command that pain and conflict cease,
 And turn to music every jarring sound.

How longs each pulse within the weary soul
  To taste the life of this benignant hour,
To be at one with thine untroubled Whole,
  And in itself to know thy hushing power.

Prepare, O Truth Supreme! through shame and pain
  A heart attuned to thy celestial calm;
Let not reflection's pangs be roused in vain,
  But heal the wounded breast with soothing balm.

So, firm in steadfast hope, in thought secure,
  In full accord to all thy world of joy,
May I be nerved to labors high and pure,
  And Thou thy child to do thy work employ.

In One, who walk'd on earth a man of wo,
  Was holier peace than e'en this hour inspires;
From Him to me let inward quiet flow,
  And give the might my failing will requires.

So this great All around, so He, and Thou,
  The central source and awful bound of things,
May fill my heart with rest as deep as now
  To land, and sea, and air, thy presence brings.

STERLING.

THE FIRE OF DRIFT-WOOD.

WE sat within the farm-house old,
  Whose windows, looking o'er the bay,
Gave to the sea-breeze, damp and cold,
  An easy entrance, night and day.

Not far away we saw the port, —
  The strange, old-fashioned, silent town, —
The light-house, — the dismantled fort, —
  The wooden houses, quaint and brown.

We sat and talked until the night,
  Descending, filled the little room;
Our faces faded from the sight,
  Our voices only broke the gloom.

We spake of many a vanished scene,
  Of what we once had thought and said,
Of what had been, and might have been,
  And who was changed, and who was dead;

And all that fills the hearts of friends,
  When first they feel, with secret pain,
Their lives thenceforth have separate ends,
  And never can be one again;

The first slight swerving of the heart,
  That words are powerless to express,
And leave it still unsaid in part,
  Or say it in too great excess.

The very tones in which we spake
  Had something strange, I could but mark;
The leaves of memory seemed to make
  A mournful rustling in the dark.

Oft died the words upon our lips,
  As suddenly, from out the fire
Built of the wrecks of stranded ships,
  The flames would leap and then expire.

And, as their splendor flashed and failed,
  We thought of wrecks upon the main, —
Of ships dismasted, that were hailed
  And sent no answer back again.

The windows, rattling in their frames, —
  The ocean, roaring up the beach, —
The gusty blast, — the bickering flames, —
  All mingled vaguely in our speech;

Until they made themselves a part
  Of fancies floating through the brain,—
The long-lost ventures of the heart,
  That send no answers back again.

O flames that glowed! O hearts that yearned!
  They were indeed too much akin,
The drift-wood fire without that burned,
  The thoughts that burned and glowed within.

H. W. Longfellow.

THE EVENING TALK.

We sat by the fisher's cottage,
  We looked on sea and sky,
We saw the mists of evening
  Come riding and rolling by:

The lights in the light-house window
  Brighter and brighter grew,
And on the dim horizon
  A ship still hung in view.

We spoke of storm and shipwreck,
  Of the seaman's anxious life;
How he floats 'twixt sky and water,
  'Twixt joy and sorrow's strife:

We spoke of coasts far distant,
  We spoke of south and north,
Strange men, and stranger customs,
  That those wild lands send forth:

Of the giant trees of Ganges,
  Whose balm perfumes the breeze;
And the fair and slender creatures,
  That kneel by the lotus-trees.

The maidens listened earnestly,
  At last the tales were ended;
The ship was gone, the dusky night
  Had on our talk descended.

From the German of HEINE.

THE TEAR.

THE latest light of evening
  Upon the waters shone,
And still we sat in the lonely hut,
  In silence and alone.

The sea-fog grew, the screaming mew
  Rose on the water's swell,
And silently in her gentle eye
  Gathered the tears and fell.

I saw them stand on the lily hand,
  Upon my knee I sank,
And, kneeling there, from her fingers fair
  The precious dew I drank.

And sense and power, since that sad hour,
  In longing waste away;
Ah me! I fear, in each witching tear
  Some subtle poison lay.

From the German of HEINE.

TWILIGHT.

The twilight is sad and cloudy,
  The wind blows wild and free,
And like the wings of sea-birds
  Flash the white caps of the sea.

But in the fisherman's cottage
  There shines a ruddier light,
And a little face at the window
  Peers out into the night.

Close, close it is pressed to the window,
  As if those childish eyes
Were looking into the darkness,
  To see some form arise.

And a woman's waving shadow
  Is passing to and fro,
Now rising to the ceiling,
  Now bowing and bending low.

What tale do the roaring ocean,
  And the night-wind, bleak and wild,
As they beat at the crazy casement,
  Tell to that little child?

And why do the roaring ocean,
  And the night-wind, wild and bleak,
As they beat at the heart of the mother,
  Drive the color from her cheek?

H. W. LONGFELLOW.

SEE where, upon the blue and waveless deep,
Comes forth the silent Moon!
Now, Music, wake from out thy charméd sleep;
And bid thy sweet soul weep
Her life away in some immortal tune!
Or let thy soaring spirit run
Aloft upon some wild enchanted air,
Before whose breath despair
Dies, like a mist before the uprisen sun!

BARRY CORNWALL.

THE FISHERMEN.

THREE fishers went sailing out into the West,
  Out into the West as the sun went down,
Each thought of the woman who loved him the best,
  And the children stood watching them out of the town;
For men must work, and women must weep,
And there 's little to earn, and many to keep,
    Though the harbor bar be moaning.

Three wives sat up in the light-house tower
  And trimmed the lamps as the sun went down,
And they looked at the squall, and they looked at the
      shower,
  And the rack it came rolling up, ragged and brown;
But men must work, and women must weep,
Though storms be sudden, and waters deep,
    And the harbor bar be moaning.

Three corpses lay out on the shining sands
  In the morning gleam as the tide went down,
And the women are watching and wringing their hands,
  For those who will never come back to the town;
For men must work, and women must weep,—
And the sooner it 's over, the sooner to sleep—
    And good bye to the bar and its moaning.

CHARLES KINGSLEY.

MOONRISE.

Above the headlands massy, dim,
  A swelling glow, a fiery birth,
A marvel in the sky doth swim,
  Advanced upon the hush of earth.

The globe, o'erhanging bright and brave
  The pale green-glimmering ocean-floor,
Silvers its wave, its rustling wave
  Soft folded on the shelving shore.

O lonely moon, a lonely place
Is this thou cheerest with thy face;
Three sand-side houses, and afar
The steady beacon's faithful star!

William Allingham.

GLIDE ON, MY BARK.

Glide on, my bark; the summer's tide
Is gently flowing to thy side;
Around thy prow, the waters bright,
In circling rounds of broken light,
Are glittering, as if ocean gave
Her countless gems to deck the wave;
Whilst moonlight shines like mimic day—
Glide on, my bark, thy moonlit way.

Glide on, my bark! how sweet to rove,
With such a beaming sky above,
O'er the dark sea, whose murmurs seem,
Like fairy music in a dream;
No sound is heard to break the spell,
Except the water's gentle swell;
Whilst midnight, like a mimic day,
Shines on, to guide our moonlit way.

Anonymous.

THE EVENING STAR.

Just above yon sandy bar,
  As the day grows fainter and dimmer,
Lonely and lovely, a single star
  Lights the air with a dusky glimmer.

Into the ocean faint and far
  Falls the trail of its golden splendor,
And the gleam of that single star
  Is ever refulgent, soft, and tender.

Chrysaor rising out of the sea,
  Showed thus glorious and thus emulous,
Leaving the arms of Callirrhoe,
  For ever tender, soft, and tremulous.

Thus o'er the ocean faint and far
  Trailed the gleam of his falchion brightly;
Is it a God, or is it a star
  That, entranced, I gaze on nightly!

H. W. Longfellow.

'THE SEA HATH ITS PEARLS.'

THE sea hath its pearls,
  The heaven hath its stars;
But my heart, my heart,
  My heart hath its love.

Great are the sea and the heaven;
  Yet greater is my heart,
And fairer than pearls and stars,
  Flashes and beams my love.

Thou little, youthful maiden,
  Come unto my great heart;
My heart and the sea, and the heaven
  Are melting away with love.

From the German of HEINE.

'WHEN STARS ARE IN THE QUIET SKIES.'

I.

WHEN stars are in the quiet skies,
  Then most I pine for thee;
Bend on me then thy tender eyes,
  As stars look on the sea.
For thoughts, like waves that glide by night,
  Are stillest when they shine,
Mine earthly love lies hush'd in light
  Beneath the heaven of thine.

II.

There is an hour when angels keep
  Familiar watch o'er men,
When coarser souls are wrapped in sleep —
  Sweet spirit, meet me then.
There is an hour when holy dreams
  Through slumber fairest glide,
And in that mystic hour it seems
  Thou shouldst be by my side.

III.

The thoughts of thee too sacred are
  For daylight's common beam;
I can but know thee as my star,
  My angel and my dream!
When stars are in the quiet skies,
  Then most I pine for thee;
Bend on me then thy tender eyes,
  As stars look on the sea.

E. L. Bulwer.

'BY THE MARGENT OF THE SEA.'

By the margent of the sea
  I would rear myself a home;
Where the mighty waters be,
  On the edges of their foam.
Ribs of sand should be the mounds
In my grounds;
My grasses should be ocean-weeds,
Strung with pulpy beads;
And my blossoms should be shells,
  Bleaching white,
Washed from ocean's deepest cells
  By the billows, morn and night.
Morn and night — in both their light,

Up and down the paven sand
I would tramp, while Day's great lamp
Rose or set, on sea and land;
Through a sea of vapors dark,
Glimmering, like a burning bark,
Drifting o'er its yawning tomb,
With a red and lurid gloom!
Seldom should its wake of gold
On the waters be unrolled;
Seldom its sister, chaste and white,
Lift her silver veil of light:
Neither wholly dark, nor bright,
Gray by day, and gray by night—
That's the light for me
By the margent of the sea!

From my window, when I rose
In the morning, I would mark
The gray sea in its endless throes,
And many a bark!
Brooding o'er the pallid sails,
That are naught to me and mine,
I would conjure up the gales,
Soon to draggle them in brine:
Then, my cloak about my face,
Up and down the sands I'd pace,
Making foot-prints for the spray
To wash away.
Waves might break along the shore,
And thunders roar;

Not for me, that hear aghast,
The solemn moaning of the Past!
Wrecks might line the wasteful sand,
Treasures heaped on every hand; —
I should only, — ah ! that only!
Is there anything so lonely? —
See the golden argosie
Which, in youth, went down with me!
And if storms should come, and rain
  Pour in torrents down the sky —
  What care I?
What cares any one in pain?
  Are not tears still wrung from me?
Woe is me! and all in vain;
Falling faster than the rain,
  In the sea!
But they would be over then,
  And I would no longer weep;
Grief is for the sea of men;
  By God's ocean it must sleep!
Happy, happy would I be,
By the margent of the sea!

Up and down the barren beaches;
  Round the ragged belts of land;
In along the curving reaches;
  Out along the horns of sand;
Over the ledges of the rocks,
Where the surges comb their locks,
And their wreathed buds remain,
Not to bloom again —

Many a league and hour I'd stray,
And brave the madness of the spray!
  The caverns in its hollow wall;
Its flame-like currents mounting slow;
Its rounding crest of frothy snow;
  Its crumbling fall;
The climbing sun, in light betrayed,
By a cloud of thinner shade;
The tossing foam, the wandering plain
Of the melancholy main;
The sea-mew darting everywhere,
Now in the water, and now in the air,
Vexing me with frantic scream,
Like a phantom in a dream —
  In dreams I do behold them all!
But hardly know, so strange they seem,
  With such thoughts combined,
Whether I behold them there, —
Or the sorrow, and despair,
  The restless ocean in my desolated mind!

R. H. Stoddard.

THEKLA'S LAMENT.

The night-clouds hurry, the forests moan,
There strays by the sea-shore a maiden lone,
The billows are breaking with might, with might,
And she flings out her voice to the darksome night; —
Her eyelids heavy with weeping.

My heart is deadened, the world is void,
No more it giveth worth being enjoyed;
Thou Holy One! summon thy child to Thee —
All the bliss of the world hath been granted to me,
In the bliss of living and loving.

From the German of Schiller.

I stretch my arms out to the heaving sea;
It heaves, and swells, and throbs with passionate pain;
Wilt thou not rise from these blue depths to me,
Thou sole beloved of this heart and brain?

Ah! vain the promise of these stately tides;
Their surging depths of unseen wonder vain;
If no wild spell within their might resides,
To give back thee, O loved and lost, again!

Anonymous.

INVOCATION.

HEAR, sweet spirit, hear the spell
Lest a blacker charm compel!
So shall the midnight breezes swell
With thy deep, long-lingering knell.

And at evening evermore,
In a chapel on the shore,
Shall the chanters, sad and saintly,
Yellow tapers burning faintly,
Doleful masses chant for thee;
    Miserere Domine!

Hark! the cadence dies away
On the quiet moonlit sea:
The boatman rest their oars and say
    Miserere Domine!

COLERIDGE.

Break, break, break,
  On thy cold gray stones, O sea!
And I would that my tongue could utter
  The thoughts that arise in me

O well for the fisherman's boy,
  That he shouts with his sister at play!
O well for the sailor lad,
  That he sings in his boat on the bay!

And the stately ships go on
  To their haven under the hill;
But O for the touch of a vanish'd hand,
  And the sound of a voice that is still!

Break, break, break,
  At the foot of thy crags, O sea!
But the tender grace of a day that is dead
  Will never come back to me.

A. Tennyson.

SONG ON THE WATER.

I.

WILD with passion, sorrow-beladen,
  Bend the thought of thy stormy soul
On its home, on its heaven, the loved maiden;
  And peace shall come at her eyes' control.
Even so night's starry rest possesses
  With its gentle spirit these tamed waters,
And bids the wave, with weedy tresses
  Embower the ocean's pavement stilly
  Where the sea-girls lie, the mermaid-daughters,
    Whose eyes, not born to weep,
    More palely-lidded sleep,
  Than in our fields the lily;
    And sighing in their rest
      More sweet than is its breath;
      And quiet as its death
        Upon a lady's breast.

II.

Heart high-beating, triumph-bewreathed,
  Search the record of loves gone by,
And borrow the blessings by them bequeathed
  To deal from out of thy victory's sky.

Even so, throughout the midnight deep,
  The silent moon doth seek the bosoms
Of those dear mermaid-girls asleep,
  To feed its dying rays anew,
Like to the bee on earthly blossoms,
    Upon their silvery whiteness,
    And on the rainbow brightness
  Of their eyelashes' dew,
    And kisseth their limbs o'er:
      Her lips where they do quaff
      Strike starry tremors off,
        As from the waves our oar.

T. L. Beddoes.

PEARL-SEED.

Songs are sung in my mind
  As pearls are formed in the sea,
Each thought with thy name entwined
  Becomes a sweet song in me.

Dimly those pale pearls shine,
  Hidden under the sea, —
Vague are those songs of mine,
  So deeply they lie in me.

George W. Curtis.

12

QUEEN MAB'S PALACE.

If solitude hath ever led thy steps
To the wild ocean's echoing shore,
And thou hast lingered there,
Until the sun's broad orb
Seemed resting on the burnished wave,
Thou must have marked the lines
Of purple gold, that motionless
Hung o'er the sinking sphere :
Thou must have marked the billowy clouds
Edged with intolerable radiancy,
Towering like rocks of jet
Crowned with a diamond wreath.
And yet there is a moment,
When the sun's highest point
Peeps like a star o'er ocean's western edge,
When those far clouds of feathery gold,
Shaded with deepest purple, gleam
Like islands on a dark blue sea ;
Then has thy fancy soared above the earth,
And furled its wearied wing
Within the Fairy's fane.

Yet not the golden islands
Gleaming in yon flood of light,
Nor the feathery curtains
Stretching o'er the sun's bright couch,
Nor the burnished ocean-waves,
Paving that gorgeous dome,
So fair, so wonderful a sight
As Mab's ethereal palace could afford.
Yet likest evening's vault, that fairy hall!
As heaven, low resting on the wave, it spread
Its floors of flashing light,
Its vast and azure dome,
Its fertile golden islands
Floating on a silver sea;
Whilst suns their mingling beamings darted
Through clouds of circumambient darkness,
And pearly battlements around
Looked o'er the immense of heaven.

SHELLEY.

NIGHT AND DEATH.

The storm-wind is howling
  Through old pines afar;
The drear night is falling
  Without moon or star.

The roused sea is lashing
  The bold shore behind,
And the moan of its ebbing
  Keeps time with the wind.

On, on through the darkness,
  A spectre, I pass
Where, like moaning of broken hearts,
  Surges the grass!

I see her lone headstone —
  'T is white as a shroud;
Like a pall hangs above it
  The low drooping cloud.

Who speaks through the dark night,
  And lull of the wind?
'T is the sound of the pine-leaves
  And sea-waves behind!

The dead girl is silent—
  I stand by her now,
And her pulse beats no quicker,
  Nor crimsons her brow.

The small hand that trembled
  When last in my own,
Lies patient and folded,
  And colder than stone.

Like the white blossoms falling
  To-night in the gale,
So she in her beauty
  Sank mournful and pale.

Yet I loved her! I utter
  Such words by her grave,
As I would not have spoken
  Her last breath to save.

Of *her* love the angels
  In heaven might tell,
While mine would be whispered
  With shudders in hell!

'T was well that the white ones,
Who bore her to bliss,
Shut out from her new life
The visions of this;

Else, sure as I stand here,
And speak of my love,
She would leave for my darkness
Her glory above.

Elizabeth H. Whittier.

THE ECHO SPIRIT.

Chequered with woven shadows as I lay
Among the grass watching the watery gleam,
I saw an echo-spirit in his bay,
Drowsed into silence by the noon-tide beam.
The depths heaved round his boat of shell, with sway
To Ocean's giant pulse, and the white dream,
Buoyed like the young moon on a level stream
Of greenish vapor at decline of day,
Swam airily. Watching the distant flocks
Of sea-gulls, whilst one foot in careless sweep
Touched the clear-trembling cool, with tiny shocks
Faint-circling; till at last he sank to sleep,
Lulled by the hush-song of the dreamy deep
Lap-lapping drowsily the heated rocks.

William Allingham.

CALM.

'Tis a dull, sullen day, — the dull beach o'er
In rippling curves the ebbing ocean flows;
Along each tiny crest that nears the shore
A line of soft green shadow rises, glides, and goes.

The tide recedes, — the flat smooth beach grows bare,
More faint the low sweet plashing on my ears,
Yet still I watch the dimpling shadows fair,
As each is born, glides, pauses, disappears.

What channel needs our faith, except the eyes?
God leaves no spot of earth unglorified;
Profuse and wasteful, lovelinesses rise;
New beauties dawn before the old have died.

Trust thou thy joys in keeping of the Power
Who holds these faint soft shadows in His hand;
Believe and live, and know that hour by hour
Will ripple newer beauty to thy strand.

Anonymous.

THE EXILE.

The swallow with summer
Will wing o'er the seas,
The wind that I sigh to
Will visit thy trees,
The ship that it hastens
Thy ports will contain,
But me — I must never
See England again!

There's many that weep there,
But one weeps alone,
For the tears that are falling
So far from her own;
So far from thy own, love.
We know not our pain;
If death is between us,
Or only the main.

When the white cloud reclines
On the verge of the sea,
I fancy the white cliffs,
And dream upon thee;

But the cloud spreads its wings
  To the blue heaven and flies.
We never shall meet, love,
  Except in the skies!

HOOD.

THE TWO OCEANS.

Two seas amid the night
  In the moonshine roll and sparkle,
Now spread in the silver light,
  Now sadden, and wail, and darkle.

The one has a billowy motion,
  And from land to land it gleams;
The other is Sleep's wide ocean,
  And its glimmering waves are dreams.

The one with murmur and roar
  Bears fleets round coast and islet;
The other, without a shore,
  Ne'er knew the track of a pilot.

STERLING.

EBB AND FLOW.

I WALKED beside the evening sea,
And dreamed a dream that could not be,
The waves that plunged along the shore,
Said only: 'dreamer, dream no more.'

But still the legions charged the beach,
And rang their battle-cry, like speech;
But changed was the imperial strain;
It murmured: 'dreamer, dream again.'

I homeward turned from out the gloom,
That sound I heard not in my room,
But suddenly a sound that stirred
Within my very breast, I heard.

It was my heart, that like a sea
Within my breast beat ceaselessly,
But like the waves along the shore,
It said 'dream on,' and 'dream no more.'

GEORGE W. CURTIS.

Ask me no more: the moon may draw the sea;
  The cloud may stoop from heaven and take the shape,
  With fold to fold, of mountain and of cape;
But, O too fond, when have I answered thee?
                    Ask me no more.

Ask me no more: what answer could I give?
  I love not hollow cheek or faded eye:
  Yet, O my friend, I will not have thee die!
Ask me no more, lest I should bid thee live;
                    Ask me no more.

Ask me no more: thy fate and mine are sealed:
  I strove against the stream, and all in vain:
  Let the great river take me to the main:
No more, dear love, for at a touch I yield;
                    Ask me no more.

Alfred Tennyson.

ANNABEL LEE.

It was many and many a year ago,
  In a kingdom by the sea;
That a maiden lived, whom you may know
  By the name of Annabel Lee;
And this maiden she lived with no other thought,
  Than to love, and be loved by me.

I was a child and she was a child
  In this kingdom by the sea;
But we loved with a love that was more than love,
  I and my Annabel Lee —
With a love that the winged seraphs of heaven
  Coveted her and me.

And this was the reason that, long ago,
  In this kingdom by the sea,
A wind blew out of a cloud, chilling
  My beautiful Annabel Lee;
So that her high-born kinsman came,
  And bore her away from me,
To shut her up in a sepulchre
  In this kingdom by the sea.

The angels, not half so happy in heaven,
  Went envying her and me.
Yes! that was the reason (as all men know)
  In this kingdom by the sea,
That the wind came out of the cloud by night,
  Chilling and killing my Annabel Lee.

But our love it was stronger by far than the love
  Of those who were older than we,
  Of many far wiser than we;
And neither the angels in heaven above,
  Nor the demons down under the sea,
Can ever dissever my soul from the soul
  Of the beautiful Annabel Lee.

For the moon never beams without bringing me dreams
  Of the beautiful Annabel Lee,
And the stars never rise, but I feel the bright eyes
  Of the beautiful Annabel Lee.
And so, all the night-tide I lie down by the side
Of my darling, my darling, my life, and my bride,
  In her sepulchre there by the sea,
  In her tomb by the sounding sea.

Edgar A. Poe.

BERTHA.

THE leaves have fallen from the trees;
For under them grew the buds of May,
And such is Nature's constant way;
Let us accept the work of her hand.
Still, if the winds sweep bare the height,
Something is left for hearts' delight,
Let us but know and understand.

Bertha looked down from the rocky cliff,
Whose feet the tender foam-wreaths kist,
Toward the outer circle of mist
That hedged the old and wonderful sea.
Below her, as if with endless hope,
Up the beach's marbled slope,
The waters clomb eternally.

Many a long-bleached sail in sight
Hovered awhile, then flitted away,
Beyond the opening of the bay;
Fair Bertha entered her cottage late,
'He does not come,' she said, and smiled,
'But the shore is dark and the sea is wild,
And, dearest father, we still must wait.'

She hastened to her inner room,
And silently mused there alone ;
'Three springs have come, three winters gone,
And still we wait from hour to hour ;
But earth waits long for her harvest-time,
And the aloe, in the northern clime,
Waits an hundred years for its flower.

'Under the apple-boughs as I sit
In May-time, when the robin's song
Thrills the odorous winds along,
The innermost heaven seems to ope ;
I think, though the old joys pass from sight,
Still something is left for hearts' delight,
For life is endless, and so is hope.

'If the aloe waits an hundred years,
And God's times are so long indeed
For simple things, as flower and weed,
That gather only the light and gloom,
For what great treasures of joy and dole,
Of life and death, perchance, must the soul,
Ere it flower in heavenly peace, find room ?

'I see that all things wait in trust,
As feeling afar God's distant ends,
And unto every creature he sends
That measure of good that fills its scope ;
The marmot enters the stiffening mould,
And the worm its dark sepulchral fold,
To hide there with its beautiful hope.'

Still Bertha waited on the cliff,
To catch the gleam of a coming sail
And the distant whisper of the gale,
Winging the unforgotten home ;
And hope at her yearning heart would knock,
When a sunbeam on a far-off rock
Married a wreath of wandering foam.

Was it well ? you ask — (nay, was it ill ?) —
Who sat last year by the old man's hearth ; —
The sun had passed below the earth,
And the first star locked its western gate,
When Bertha entered his darkening home,
And smiling said, 'He does not come,
But, dearest father, we still can wait !'

Anne Whitney.

HOPES AND WAVES.

HOPES on hopes from the bosom sever,
But the heart hopes on, unchanging ever;
Wave after wave breaks on the shore,
But the sea is deep as it was before.

That the billows heave with a ceaseless motion
Is the very life of the throbbing ocean;
And hopes that from day to day upstart
Are the swelling wave-beats of the heart.

From the German of RÜCKERT.

MY hopes retire, my wishes as before
Struggle to find their resting-place, in vain:
The ebbing sea thus beats against the shore;
The shore repels it; it returns again.

W. S. LANDOR.

WRITING ON THE SANDS.

I PAUSED at early morn to trace
My name upon the sand,
Nor cared to think how soon the race
Of leaping waters would efface
The record of my hand.

But now the broad'ning blue expanse
Rolls higher up the shore;
Farther the curling waves advance, —
Their smiles of light, their wreathed dance
Are nearer than before.

And now, — alas that human pride
So slight a thing may quell!
With yonder words beneath the tide,
I feel that all I've wrought beside
May disappear as well.

And dare I deem that all this strife
Of thoughts within my soul,
These hopes with which my heart is rife,
These longings for a glorious life,
Will find a better goal?

Oh, coward! when the trumpet's call
  Is sounding in thy heart,
Pause not to basely reckon all
The risks to triumph or to fall,
  But forth — and act thy part!

I know not if the bearded grain
  Or barren stalks await
Mine autumn hours. Yet not in vain
The toil, though God the fruits restrain
  Or grant the harvest late.

Oh Love, that askest but to be!
  Oh Faith, that will not die!
Life, courage, strength, ye are to me,
While all things change, and fade, and flee,
  In ocean, earth, and sky.

W. H. Hurlbut.

My life is like a stroll upon the beach,
  As near the ocean's edge as I can go;
My tardy steps its waves sometimes o'erreach,
  Sometimes I stay to let them overflow.

My sole employment 'tis, and scrupulous care
  To set my gains beyond the reach of tides,
Each smoother pebble and each shell more rare,
  Which ocean kindly to my hand confides.

I have but few companions on the shore,
  They scorn the strand who sail upon the sea;
Yet oft I think the ocean they've sailed o'er,
  Is deeper known upon the strand to me.

The middle sea contains no crimson dulse,
  Its deeper waves cast up no pearls to view,
Along the shore my hand is on its pulse,
  And I converse with many a shipwrecked crew.

H. D. Thoreau.

The sad rhyme of the men who proudly clung
To their first fault, and wither'd in their pride.

Over the sea our galleys went,
With cleaving prows in order brave,
To a speeding wind and a bounding wave —
A gallant armament:
Each bark built out of a forest-tree,
Left leafy and rough as first it grew,
And nail'd all over the gaping sides,
Within and without, with black-bull hides,
Seeth'd in fat and suppled in flame,
To bear the playful billows' game;
So each good ship was rude to see,
Rude and bare to the outward view,
But each upbore a stately tent;
Where cedar-pales in scented row
Kept out the flakes of the dancing brine:
And an awning drooped the mast below,
In fold on fold of the purple fine,
That neither noon-tide, nor star-shine,
Nor moonlight cold which maketh mad,
Might pierce the regal tenement,

When the sun dawn'd, oh, gay and glad
We set the sail and plied the oar;
But when the night-wind blew like breath,
For joy of one day's voyage more,
We sang together on the wide sea,
Like men at peace on a peaceful shore;
Each sail was loosed to the wind so free,
Each helm made sure by the twilight star,
And in a sleep as calm as death,
We, the strangers from afar,
   Lay stretch'd along, each weary crew
In a circle round its wondrous tent,
Whence gleam'd soft light and curl'd rich scent,
   And with light and perfume, music too:
So the stars wheel'd round, and the darkness past,
And at morn we started beside the mast,
And still each ship was sailing fast!

One morn, the land appear'd! — a speck
   Dim trembling betwixt sea and sky —
Avoid it, cried our pilot, check
   The shout, restrain the longing eye!
But the heaving sea was black behind
For many a night and many a day,
And land, though but a rock, was nigh;
So we broke the cedar pales away,
Let the purple awning flap in the wind,
   And a statue bright was on every deck!
We shouted, every man of us,
And steered right into the harbor thus,
With pomp and pæan glorious.

An hundred shapes of lucid stone!
  All day we built a shrine for each —
A shrine of rock for every one —
Nor paused till in the westering sun
  We sate together on the beach
To sing, because our task was done;
When lo! what shouts and merry songs!
What laughter all the distance stirs!
What raft comes loaded with its throngs
Of gentle islanders!
'Our isles are just at hand,' they cried;
  'Like cloudlets faint at even sleeping,
Our temple-gates are open'd wide,
  Our olive-groves thick shade are keeping
For the lucid shapes you bring,' they cried.
Oh then we awoke with sudden start
From our deep dream; we knew, too late,
How bare the rock, how desolate,
To which we had flung our precious freight:
  Yet we called out — 'Depart!
Our gifts, once given, must here abide:
Our work is done; we have no heart
To mar our work,' we cried.

ROBERT BROWNING.

TO MY COMPANIONS.

Ye heavy-hearted mariners
  Who sail this shore,
Ye patient, ye who labor
  Sitting at the sweeping oar,
And see afar the flashing sea-gulls play
On the free waters, and the glad bright day
Twine with his hand the spray;
  From out your dreariness,
  From your heart-weariness,
  I speak, for I am yours
  On these gray shores.

Nay, nay, I know not, Mariners,
  What cliffs these are,
That high uplift their smooth dark fronts,
  And sadly round us bar;
I do imagine, that the free clouds play
Above those eminent heights, that somewhere Day
Rides his triumphant way,
  And hath secure dominion
  Over our stern oblivion,
  But see no path thereout
  To free from doubt.

W. E. Channing.

THE OCEAN.

——'In a season of calm weather,
Though inland far we be,
Our souls have sight of that immortal sea
That brought us hither,
Can in a moment travel thither,
And see the children sport upon the shore,
And hear the mighty waters rolling evermore.'

WORDSWORTH.

TELL me, brother, what are we? —
Spirits bathing in the sea
Of Deity!
Half afloat and half on land,
Wishing much to leave the strand, —
Standing, gazing with devotion,
Yet afraid to trust the Ocean —
Such are we.

Wanting love and holiness
To enjoy the wave's caress;
Wanting faith and heavenly hope,
Buoyantly to bear us up;
Yet impatient in our dwelling,
When we hear the ocean swelling,

And in every wave that rolls
We behold the happy souls
Peacefully, triumphantly
Swimming on the smiling sea,
Then we linger round the shore,
Lovers of the earth no more.

Once, — 'twas in our infancy,
We were drifted by this sea
To the coast of human birth,
To this body and this earth:
Gentle were the hands that bore
Our young spirits to the shore;
Gentle lips that bade us look
Outward from our cradle-nook
To the spirit-bearing ocean
With such wonder and devotion,
As each stilly Sabbath day,
We were led a little way,
Where we saw the waters swell
Far away from inland dell,
And received with grave delight
Symbols of the Infinite: —
Then our home was near the sea;
'Heaven was round our infancy:'
Night and day we heard the waves
Murmuring by as to their caves; —
Floated in unconscious life,
With no later doubts at strife,
Trustful of the upholding power
Who sustained us hour by hour.

Now we 've wandered from the shore,
Dwellers by the sea no more;
Yet at times there comes a tone
Telling of the visions flown,
Sounding from the distant sea,
Where we left our purity;
Distant glimpses of the surge
Lure us down to ocean's verge;
There we stand with vague distress,
Yearning for the measureless;
By half-wakened instincts driven,
Half-loving earth, half-loving heaven,
Fearing to put off and swim,
Yet impelled to turn to Him
In whose life we live and move,
And whose very name is Love.

Grant me courage, Holy One,
To become indeed Thy son,
And in thee, thou Parent-Sea,
Live and love eternally.

C. P. Cranch.

THE MORNING MIST.

THE mist that like a dim soft pall was lying,
  Mingling the gray sea with the low gray sky,
Floats upward now; the sunny breeze is sighing,
  And Youth stands pale before his destiny;
        O passionate heart of Youth!
  Each rolling wave with herald voice is crying,
  Thou canst delay, but never shun replying,
  It calls thee living or it calls thee dying,
Though all the beauty fade before the glare of Truth.

Thou wanderest onward 'neath the solemn morning,
  It seems like mid-day ere the sun rides high,
The soft mist fades, whose shadowy adorning
  Wrapt in a dreamy haze the earth and sky;
        The Ocean lies before!
  O thou art lost if thou discard the warning
  To make hot Day more fair than fairest dawning,
  Till Eve look back serenely on the morning
When Youth stood trembling on the ocean-shore.

T. W. HIGGINSON.

'AS SHIPS BECALMED.'

As ships becalmed at eve, that lay
  With canvas drooping, side by side,
Two towers of sail at dawn of day
  Are scarce, long leagues apart, descried;

When fell the night, upsprung the breeze,
  And all the darkling hours they plied,
Nor dreamt but each the self-same seas
  By each was cleaving, side by side; —

Even so — but why the tale reveal
  Of those whom, year by year unchanged,
Brief absence joined anew to feel,
  Astounded, soul from soul estranged?

At dead of night their sails were filled,
  And onward each rejoicing steered:
Ah, neither blame, for neither willed
  Or wist, what first with dawn appeared.

To veer, how vain! On, onward strain,
  Brave barks! In light, in darkness too,
Through winds and tides one compass guides,—
  To that, and your own selves, be true.

But O blithe breeze! and O great seas!
  Though ne'er, that earliest parting past,
On your wide plain they join again,
  Together lead them home at last!

One port, methought, alike they sought,
  One purpose hold where'er they fare:—
O bounding breeze, O rushing seas!
  At last, at last, unite them there!

A. H. Clough.

THE END.

www.ingramcontent.com/pod-product-compliance
Lightning Source LLC
LaVergne TN
LVHW050530100826
845148LV00002B/512

* 9 7 8 1 4 2 5 5 1 9 1 7 9 *